TIMESAVER FOR EXAMS

IELTS Grammar

(5.5–7.5)

By Fiona Davis

Contents

PHOTOCOPIABLE

Introduction

Who is this book for?

This book is for teachers of students preparing for the Academic version of the IELTS test, and who are aiming for a score of 6.0 – 7.5. It is an ideal supplement to any IELTS preparation coursebook, especially for students who already have a good grounding in English. The topics and activities reflect those typical of the IELTS Academic test and are designed especially to appeal to young adults. This resource is also suitable for use with any upper-intermediate or advanced classes who wish to extend their knowledge of English grammar, especially with a view to academic study.

The IELTS test: an overview

The International English Language Testing System (IELTS) is a test that measures the language proficiency of people who want to study or work in environments where English is used as a language of communication. An easy-to-use 9-band scale clearly identifies proficiency level, from non-user (band score 1) through to expert (band score 9).

IELTS is available in two test formats – Academic or General Training – and provides a valid and accurate assessment of the four language skills: listening, reading, writing and speaking. This Timesaver title focuses on the Academic version of the test.

There are four components to the test.

Reading   60 minutes.
There are three texts with 40 questions.

Writing   60 minutes.
There are two writing tasks. Task 1 has a minimum of 150 words. Task 2 has a minimum of 250 words.

Listening   30 minutes (plus 10 minutes for transferring answers).
There are four sections with 40 questions.

Speaking   11-14 minutes.
There are three parts.

Scoring
Each component of the test is given a band score. The average of the four scores produces the overall band score. You do not pass or fail IELTS; you receive a score.

The IELTS scale

BAND SCORE	SKILL LEVEL	DESCRIPTION
9	Expert user	The test taker has fully operational command of the language. Their use of English is appropriate, accurate and fluent, and shows complete understanding.
8	Very good user	The test taker has fully operational command of the language with only occasional unsystematic inaccuracies and inappropriate usage. They may misunderstand some things in unfamiliar situations. They handle complex and detailed argumentation well.
7	Good user	The test taker has operational command of the language, though with occasional inaccuracies, inappropriate usage and misunderstandings in some situations. They generally handle complex language well and understand detailed reasoning.
6	Competent user	The test taker has an effective command of the language despite some inaccuracies, inappropriate usage and misunderstandings. They can use and understand fairly complex language, particularly in familiar situations.
5	Modest user	The test taker has a partial command of the language and copes with overall meaning in most situations, although they are likely to make many mistakes. They should be able to handle basic communication in their own field.
4	Limited user	The test taker's basic competence is limited to familiar situations. They frequently show problems in understanding and expression. They are not able to use complex language.
3	Extremely limited user	The test taker conveys and understands only general meaning in very familiar situations. There are frequent breakdowns in communication.
2	Intermittent user	The test taker has great difficulty understanding spoken and written English.
1	Non-user	The test taker has no ability to use the language except a few isolated words.

For full details on the IELTS test, go to: **www.ielts.org**

How do I use this book?

Use the lessons to supplement your IELTS preparation coursebook by providing extra practice of key upper-intermediate and advanced-level grammar. The grammar structures have been chosen for their relevance to the IELTS exam and are representative of the more formal and impersonal style that is found in academic English. Each lesson begins with a Check Your Grammar activity to familiarise students with the target structure before they move on to more complex applications. Teachers can use the Check Your Grammar exercise as a diagnostic tool. Students will need to be confident in the language in the Check Your Grammar section before approaching the later tasks.

A variety of IELTS text types provide examples of key grammar items in context, accompanied by exam task types and exercises. Each lesson contains a concise Grammar reference with a deductive style approach and a number of examples to help with understanding. Follow-up exercises give students the opportunity to practise the key grammar in typical academic contexts and through exam tasks.

- Contents page lists grammatical focus, skill and IELTS question type for each lesson
- Each lesson covers between 80 and 100 minutes of class time, depending on class size and language level. If the lesson contains a Writing essay task (Task 2), it is assumed that students will plan the essay in class and complete it for homework.
- The comprehensive answer key provides full explanation of the answers.
- Some activities include pair and groupwork to expand students' use of the language. These can be adapted depending on context and class size.
- Grammar and exam tips in each lesson help students to avoid common errors and provide advice on academic language use.
- Lessons are designed to be teacher-led with clear instructions on the pages, which are all photocopiable.

How important is grammar to exam success?

The IELTS test does not contain any tasks which specifically test grammar. However, a successful candidate aiming for a high band score will need to have a solid and confident command of grammar, both productively and receptively. In the Writing and Speaking tests, half of the overall score is based on grammatical range and accuracy, along with coherence and fluency / cohesion.

The lessons which contain exam tasks from the Academic Reading and Academic Writing tests allow students to practise the grammar structures in relevant tasks. Examples of the key grammar appear in contexts that are appropriate for the exam and at a similar level of complexity to the passages in the Reading paper. Information is also presented through graphs, diagrams and charts, familiarising students with data interpretation. The grammar structures will help students to organise and express their ideas accurately in both tasks of the Writing test.

A successful candidate in the Speaking test must demonstrate accurate use of a wide range of structures, when expressing, justifying and discussing opinions. Speaking activities and exam tasks in this book focus on key structures and give students the opportunity to practise these skills and expand the range of their spoken language.

The Timesaver series

The Timesaver series provides hundreds of ready-made lessons for all language levels and age groups, covering skills work, language practice and cross-curricular and cross-cultural material. See the full range of print and digital resources at: **www.scholastic.co.uk/elt**

The evolution of cephalopods

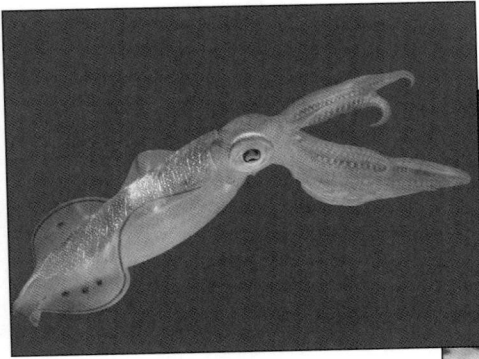
squid

octopus

cuttlefish

1a Cephalopods are a group of animals which includes squid, octopus and cuttlefish. Work in pairs. Which of these statements do you think are true of cephalopods?

a) Cephalopods are invertebrates.

b) Many cephalopods are endangered.

c) Some species are intelligent.

d) An individual cephalopod lives for many years.

1b Read this article about cephalopods from a science journal and check your answers.

Humans have changed the world's oceans in ways that have been catastrophic for many marine species. However, according to new evidence, it certainly (**1**) *appears / is appearing* that the change has so far been good for cephalopods, a group of marine invertebrates, including squid. A recent study shows that numbers of cephalopods (**2**) *have been rising / have risen* for a few years and the trend (**3**) *seems / is seeming* likely to continue. The Environment Institute at the University of Adelaide in Australia funded the study which involved researchers all over the world.

Researchers already know that cephalopods, particularly the *Coleoidea*

subclass (cuttlefish, squid and octopuses) are intelligent, grow rapidly and have short lifespans, meaning they can adapt to changes in conditions more quickly than many other marine species.

Scientists (**4**) *are now investigating / now investigate* the factors responsible for the increase in cephalopods and the impact of this on other species as well as the benefits there could be for human communities who rely on them as a resource. This research could also enable scientists to find out exactly how the ocean (**5**) *changes / is changing* as a result of current human activities.

2 **Check your grammar!** Work in pairs. Circle the correct verb form for items 1–5 in the text in exercise 1b.

3 Circle the correct words *in italics* to complete the definitions. Use the examples in the text in exercise 1b to help you.

a) Progressive verb forms (also called *continuous / perfect* tenses) are formed with *be + -ing*.

b) We often use progressive forms to emphasise that a situation is *ongoing / complete* or *temporary / permanent*.

c) Some verbs are never or rarely used in progressive forms. These verbs are sometimes known as *state / active* verbs and describe *an unchanging state / an action*.

4 Match the headings in the word box to the lists in the Grammar reference.

> Description   Mental process verbs   Possession   Preferences and feelings   Use of senses

---

Grammar reference: state verbs

State verbs are not often used in progressive forms. Some common examples of state verbs are:

a) ....

feel, hear, see, smell, sound, taste

b) ....

adore, despise, (dis)like, enjoy, hate, hope, love, mind, need, prefer, regret, want, wish

c) ....

appear, consist of, contain, differ from, fit, include, involve, look, mean, resemble, seem, weigh

d) ....

(dis)agree (= (not) have the same opinion), anticipate, appreciate, assume, believe, consider, doubt, expect, feel (= have an opinion), find, forget, imagine, know, realise, recognise, remember, see (= understand), suppose, think (= have an opinion), understand

e) ....

belong to, have, own, possess

- Some state verbs can have a progressive form with a different meaning. The progressive form generally describes an action rather than a state, e.g. *Find out what your partner **thinks** (state). What **are** you **thinking** about? (action) **Do** you **have** a stomach-ache? (state) **Are** you **having** a party this weekend? (action)*. Other common examples are: *anticipate, appear, expect, feel, imagine, see, smell, taste, weigh*.

- Occasionally state verbs are used in progressive forms to emphasise the idea of something happening at the time of speaking or something which is developing. This is particularly true of verbs that describe feelings and mental processes, e.g. *They are hoping to carry out further research. We are realising how much these creatures can teach us.*

- The meaning of *can* used with *see, hear, feel, taste, smell, remember* and *understand* is similar to a progressive meaning, e.g. *Can you smell something?*

- State verbs may use *-ing* forms in other kinds of structure, e.g. *Researchers already know that cephalopods grow rapidly, meaning (= which means) they can adapt more quickly than many other marine species.*

---

5 Complete the sentences with a simple or progressive form of the verb in brackets.

A resourceful predator

Biologists have long noted the similarities between the eyes of a cephalopod and the eyes of a human. Cephalopod eyes

(1) .... (resemble) those of humans since both animals have a camera-type eye, which

(2) .... (consist) of an iris and a circular lens. Although cephalopods are classified as invertebrates within the mollusc family, and many molluscs **(3)** .... (have) no brain, staring into the large eyes of an octopus has led many biologists to wonder what the creature **(4)** .... (think). This may not be as unlikely as it

(5) .... (sound) since recent studies indicate that octopuses are remarkably intelligent. Measuring the minds of other creatures is a perplexing problem. One yardstick scientists use is brain size, but size **(6)** .... (not always / mean) intelligence. Scientists can also count neurons. The common octopus has more neurons in its brain than a human and three-fifths of them are in its arms. It could be, when an octopus is wrapping her tentacles around a human's hands, that she

(7) .... (look) at you.

Octopuses are well-known for changing colour. But **(8)** .... (how / know) which colours to turn? Researchers from Woods Hole Marine Biological Laboratory and the University of Washington found that the skin of the cuttlefish *Sepia officinalis,* a colour-changing cousin of octopuses,

(9) .... (contain) gene sequences usually found only in the light-sensing retina of the eye. This evidence **(10)** .... (appear) to suggest that cephalopods

(11) .... (see) with their skin.

As humans, we **(12)** .... (like) to believe we are unique in evolutionary terms, but scientists **(13)** .... (gradually / realise) that this may not be the case. Humans – like other vertebrates whose intelligence we **(14)** .... (recognise), such as parrots, elephants and whales – are long-lived, social beings. Octopuses, however, are neither long-lived nor social and have evolved from a slow-moving, snail-like ancestor to become active, resourceful predators. Octopuses **(15)** .... (represent) the pinnacle of an evolutionary track which

(16) .... (differ) significantly from that of man. This groundbreaking research into cephalopods **(17)** .... (currently / challenge) our understanding of evolution,

(18) .... (include) our perspective on the emergence of life elsewhere in the universe.

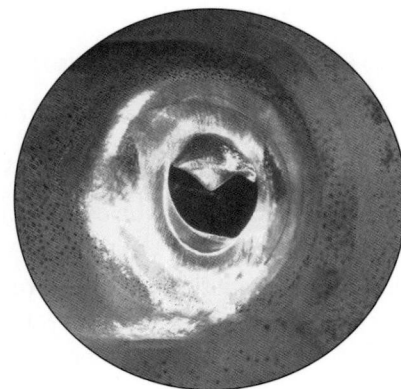

Grammar tip

To report research findings we tend to use the present simple or present perfect and not a progressive verb form, e.g. *A recent study shows / has shown …*

6 **Discuss the questions in small groups.**

a) How many of the facts about cephalopods in these texts do you think are well-known?

b) Why is our understanding of evolution being challenged by cephalopods?

c) Which physical features or aspects of the behaviour of an octopus do you think are unusual?

✎ EXAM TASK: Writing (Task 2)

7 **Write about the topic below. Give reasons for your answer and include any relevant examples from your own knowledge or experience. In your answer, try to use some of the useful phrases from the box.**

Some people feel that animals should have the same rights as humans and should not be used for either food or research. Others believe that the primary function of animals is as a food source.

Discuss both of these views and give your own opinion.

Useful phrases

Some people feel / believe …

People assume that …

…, including / involving …

It seems / appears (likely) that …

This means that …

I recognise / appreciate that …

Current research into … is leading us to question …

✎ EXAM TASK: Speaking (Part 3)

8 **Work in pairs. Discuss the questions.**

What kinds of animal are most popular in your country? Why do you think this is?

Do you think money should be spent on research into animal species?

Some species of animal are endangered due to human activity. What does this mean for the future of our planet?

Information overload

1a   **Work in pairs. Discuss the questions.**

   a) What mobile device do you use and what tasks do you use it for?

   b) When did you last go on social media and what did you do?

   c) What profile picture are you currently using? Are you happy with it?

   d) Have you ever checked social media in the middle of a class?

1b   **Check your grammar!** **What does each question ask about? Match the questions and the actions.**

   a) regular activity   **b)** an experience at an unspecified time in the past

   c) something happening now   **d)** an activity at a specified point in the past

2a   **Look at these sentences from an online news feature. What words do you think were in the original article?**

   a) There has been a dramatic .... in the amount of time we spend on our devices.

   b) A .... has found that one in four people admits to spending more time online than they spend asleep.

   c) A telecommunications company commissioned the report earlier ....

   d) The average person checks their smartphone 150 times ....

   e) Psychologists have been warning us about the risks of information overload ....

   f) Many of us are starting to show symptoms of .... addiction.

2b   **Look at the sentences again. What tenses are used in each sentence?**

3   **Read the Grammar reference and complete the information with the phrases in the box.**

- present perfect continuous
- recent studies
- leads up to now
- may be understood or implied
- give news of recent events
- which the speaker views as more long-term
- with questions beginning *How long …?*

Grammar reference: present perfect

Use the present perfect to refer to events which took place in a period of time that started in the past and
(1) .... This period of time is unfinished, e.g. *I've only had this phone since last week*. The present perfect can refer to an event that has happened once or several times, e.g. *I've had three new phones this year*.

- These events may be very recent or the speaker may feel that they are very relevant to the present. The present perfect is often used to **(2)** .... , e.g. *Scientists have discovered that modern technology may change the way our brains work.*

- Time expressions may be used, or the time period **(3)** .... by the speaker or writer, e.g. *There has been growing concern over our use of technology (over the last few years).*

- In academic essays, we can use the present perfect to refer to **(4)** .... or generally accepted theories. The present simple is also common, e.g. *A report has found … / Research shows …* (active) *It has been argued that … / It is thought that …* (passive). Use the present perfect to describe current trends and developments. This is particularly useful in a topic sentence at the start of a paragraph, e.g. *There has been a dramatic increase in the amount of time we spend on our devices.*

Present perfect simple or present perfect continuous?

- Use the present perfect continuous to place greater emphasis on the duration of the activity. The activity can be continuous or repeated and is often ongoing or has only recently stopped, e.g. *She's been checking her phone for the last half hour*. The present perfect continuous is preferred **(5)** .... , e.g. *How long has this been going on?*

- Use the present perfect simple to focus on something completed or talk about how often we have done something, e.g. *We're very pleased with the work that has been done. I've phoned her three times already!*

- Sometimes the choice of the simple or continuous form depends on the view of the speaker or writer. The **(6)** .... may be used for an event the speaker considers temporary, e.g. *I haven't been focussing on my work recently.* The simple form can be used to talk about situations **(7)** .... , e.g. *He's worked at the same place for a while.*

4 Complete the gaps in the text about information overload. Use an appropriate tense of the verb in brackets. More than one answer is sometimes possible.

For many years concern **(1)** .... *(increase)* about the stress caused by digital devices. In the workplace, technology **(2)** .... *(not / bring)* us the much anticipated reduced workload. In fact, technological innovations **(3)** .... *(set up)* even greater expectations of what can be achieved. Current research **(4)** .... *(suggest)* that information overload affects not only our personal well-being but also our productivity. A recent study **(5)** .... *(demonstrate)* that it takes people an average of twenty-five minutes to return to a work task after an email interruption.

> **Grammar tip**
>
> Some verbs are not common in the continuous form, *e.g. appear, believe, hear, know, think, seem, e.g. I haven't heard (been hearing) from him for a long time.*

Over the last few decades a number of studies **(6)** .... *(publish)* claiming that the quantity of information we receive will one day become too much. The term 'information overload' first **(7)** .... *(appear)* as long ago as 1970. Some of the claims may be exaggerated. People **(8)** .... *(complain)* about excessive information since the printing revolution in the fifteenth century. It seems unimaginable now that people in Victorian times **(9)** .... *(worry)* about the effect the invention of the telegraph had on the businessman.

Nevertheless, there are some major areas of concern about the current information age, including the effect that the information load has on our health. Receiving content in countless formats **(10)** .... *(constantly / put)* us under mental strain. Scientists **(11)** .... *(discover)* that multi-taskers produce more stress hormones. Lack of focus also effects creativity. Harvard Business School **(12)** .... *(monitor)* people's work habits for a number of years. Their ongoing research **(13)** .... *(show)* that people are more likely to be creative if they are allowed to focus without interruptions. Overload can also make workers less productive. A researcher from the University of Michigan, **(14)** .... *(prove)* that people who complete certain tasks in parallel take much longer and make more errors than people who complete the same tasks in sequence.

5 Work in pairs. Discuss the questions.

a) How many times have you checked your phone today?

b) How much time do you spend online on an average day?

c) Have you ever felt stressed by technology?

d) The concept of a digital detox has been gaining in popularity in recent years. Why do you think this is?

> **Grammar tip**
>
> In American English, the past simple is often preferred to the present perfect and is sometimes used in sentences which would not be considered correct in British English, e.g. *Did you finish yet? (US) Have you finished yet? (UK)*

6 Read the Grammar reference and the blog entry about a digital detox. Circle the present perfect or past simple in the blog. Sometimes both tenses are possible depending on how you view the events.

Grammar reference: present perfect

Present perfect or past simple?
- Some time expressions commonly associated with the present perfect are: *during/in/over the last … , in my life, lately, so far, to date, until now, since … , it's the (first) time … , … yet.*
- Some time expressions which commonly take either the present perfect or past simple, are: *already, for … , just, once, … before, recently, this (morning), today.* The past simple is used for time periods which are considered finished, and the choice of tense often depends on how the speaker or writer views the time period.

Surviving without technology 19 comments

(1) *I've recently started / I recently started* a three-week digital detox. Over the last year, **(2)** *I've become / I became* increasingly aware of how much I rely on digital devices in both my personal and professional life. As a millennial – **(3)** *I've celebrated / I celebrated* the start of the 21st century when I was still at college – **(4)** *I've been feeling / I felt* daunted by the idea of surviving without technology. Luckily, my digital detox coach **(5)** *has advised / advised me* immediately that millennials should not feel bad about their use of technology. Technology is something we **(6)** *have grown up / grew up* with.

Soon after the programme started, **(7)** *I've turned off / I turned off* notifications on my phone for all apps. **(8)** *Have I missed / Did I miss* the apps at all? If I'm honest, no. This week **(9)** *I've installed / I installed* a filter to keep my email inbox in check and **(10)** *I've reduced / I reduced* the number of times I check my emails every day. My detox **(11)** *has already given / already gave* me a feeling of being back in control. Since starting the detox two weeks ago, **(12)** *I've been sleeping / I slept* better and **(13)** *I haven't woken up / didn't wake up* to check my phone once. Today **(14)** *I've come / I came* to the conclusion that it's not about unplugging your technology but creating better habits around it. **(15)** *I've never thought / I never thought* about technology in this way before.

✎ EXAM TASK: Speaking (Part 2)

7 Prepare answers to the questions. In pairs, take turns to talk about the topic for one to two minutes.

> Describe a digital device or digital software which you find irreplaceable.
>
> You should say:
>   what the device or software is
>   how long you have been using it
>   what effect it has had on your life or the way you study
> and explain why you would recommend it to a friend.

✎ EXAM TASK: Speaking (Part 3)

8 Work in pairs. Discuss the questions.

> What effects have digital technology had on the way we work?
>
> Do companies have a responsibility to help their employees cope with information?
>
> Have you ever considered unplugging your technology?

A dream come true

1a Look at the photos and read the sentences. What is each person famous for?

The Wright brothers

Alberto Santos-Dumont

Amelia Earhart

Wiley Post

Frank Whittle

> **Grammar tip**
>
> The past perfect is used in relation to another past tense. Don't use the past perfect just to talk about something that happened a long time ago.

a) The Wright brothers *made / had made* a number of unsuccessful flights when they finally *achieved / were achieving* their first powered flight in an aeroplane on December 17th, 1903.

b) When he *built / had built* and *flew / flown* a number of powered airships, Alberto Santos-Dumont *carried out / was carrying out* the first public flight of a powered aeroplane in Europe.

c) In 1928, Amelia Earhart was the first female pilot to fly across the Atlantic. Eleven years later, she *disappeared / had disappeared* while she *attempted / was attempting* to fly round the world.

d) In 1933, Wiley Post *made / was making* history when he *became / had become* the first person to fly solo around the world in his plane, the Winnie Mae.

e) In 1935, after a few years studying engineering, Flight Lieutenant Frank Whittle *told / had told* a well-known aeronautical engineer about the idea for a jet engine he *came up with / had come up with*.

1b **Check your grammar!** Which forms of the verbs are given in the sentences? Circle the best forms.

✎ EXAM TASK: Reading (Identifying information)

2 Read the text about Alberto Santos-Dumont and the Deutsch prize on page 14. Do the following statements agree with the information given in the text? Write

TRUE if the statement agrees with the information
FALSE if the statement contradicts the information
NOT GIVEN if there is no information on this

1 Aviation was a recent passion for Alberto Santos-Dumont.

2 After the announcement of the Deutsch prize, Alberto built his first dirigible.

3 Alberto Santos-Dumont felt at home in France.

4 Air traffic control was invented by 1900.

5 Balloon No. 5 crashed into the roof of the Hotel Trocadero and then caught fire.

6 Alberto Santos-Dumont entered the race after No. 6 was ready.

In May 1900, a wealthy aviation enthusiast in Paris, Henri Deutsch de la Meurthe, announced that he had decided to offer a large prize to the first pilot of a machine capable of flying eleven kilometres to the Eiffel Tower and back in under thirty minutes. For Alberto Santos-Dumont, a Brazilian aviation pioneer who had been living in Paris for a number of years to study engineering, it was a dream come true. Alberto had been fascinated by machinery from an early age and had always wanted to fly. By 1900, Alberto was something of a celebrity in Paris, where he had mastered balloon flying and had developed a steerable, engine-driven balloon, known as a 'dirigible'. He parked his dirigible at his apartment and since no one had yet thought of air traffic control, he was known to float at rooftop level around the city and would even land near an outdoor café to have lunch.

Once he heard about the Deutsch prize, Santos-Dumont made a number of attempts to win but each failed for one reason or another. On one such attempt, Santos-Dumont's dirigible No. 5 lost hydrogen, started to descend and crashed into the roof of the Trocadero hotel. While Santos-Dumont was hanging dangerously in the balloon basket from the side of the hotel, the balloon caught fire. Santos-Dumont had to be rescued by the Paris fire brigade. However, he was not put off and built dirigible No. 6. When he had finished testing the handling of his latest balloon, Santos-Dumont set a date for his prize-winning flight.

3 **Match the timelines to the descriptions a–c in the Grammar reference below.**

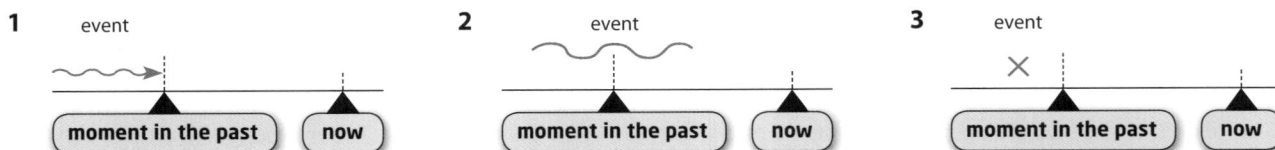

1 event
moment in the past   now

2 event
moment in the past   now

3 event
moment in the past   now

Grammar reference: past perfect

Past perfect

To talk about an event in the past that happens before another event in the past, both the past simple and the past perfect can be used. This is particularly true of sentences using time expressions such as *when*, *after*, *as soon as* or *once*, e.g. *Once he heard / had heard about the Deutsch prize, Santos-Dumont made a number of attempts to win.* (Both options could be used with little difference in meaning.)

● Use the past perfect if the order of events in a sentence is not clear without it, or to emphasise that the events are separate, e.g. *In the early 1900s, Alberto was something of a celebrity in Paris, where he had developed a steerable, engine-driven balloon.* (The past perfect emphasises that Alberto invented a steerable balloon before he achieved celebrity.)

● Use the past perfect in reported speech when the reporting verb is in the past simple, e.g. *He announced that he had decided to offer a large prize.*

● The passive of the past perfect is formed with *had + been* + past participle.

Past perfect simple or past perfect continuous?

● Use the past perfect simple to describe an event or a situation which finished before a moment in the past.

a) ....

● Use the past perfect continuous *had + been + -ing* to talk about an event or situation which continues until a moment or event in the past, e.g. *For Alberto Santos-Dumont, a Brazilian aviation pioneer who **had been living** in Paris for a number of years, it was a dream come true.* **b)** ....

Past perfect continuous or past continuous?

Use the past continuous to talk about an event or situation which was in progress at a moment in the past, e.g. *While Santos-Dumont **was hanging** dangerously in the balloon basket from the side of the hotel, the balloon caught fire.* **c)** ....

4 **Read the text and circle the correct form of the verb.**

In 1904, during a conversation with his friend, the watchmaker Louis Cartier, Alberto Santos-Dumont mentioned that he couldn't look at his watch while he **(1)** *was flying / had been flying* since he needed to keep his hands on the controls. Until then, men **(2)** *were wearing / had been wearing* a watch in their top pocket. Some women wore watches on their wrists as an item of jewellery – Queen Elizabeth I of England wore one she **(3)** *had received / had been receiving* as a present. Louis Cartier went on to design a watch with a leather band and small buckle. By the end of the decade, Cartier **(4)** *had become / had been becoming* one of the most famous watch companies in the world and you can still buy the Santos wristwatch today.

> **Grammar tip**
>
> State verbs such as *appear, be, become, doubt, prefer, want* tend not to be used in continuous forms, e.g. *He had always wanted to fly.* ~~(had always been wanting)~~

5 **Complete the account of Santos-Dumont's prize-winning flight by using the verb in brackets in an appropriate form. Sometimes more than one answer is possible.**

October 19th, 1901 was a windy day. Santos-Dumont **(1)** .... *(watch)* the weather conditions with some concern for several hours before he made the decision to go ahead. At 2.42 pm he set off in No. 6 – the sixth airship **(2)** he .... *(built)* so far – and after only nine minutes, he rounded the Eiffel Tower and **(3)** .... *(start)* the flight back. However, the engine, which **(4)** .... *(work)* well up to that point, began to falter as he **(5)** .... *(drive)* into the wind. At times Alberto **(6)** .... *(have to)* abandon the steering in order to keep the engine going and finally **(7)** .... *(cross)* the finish line to the gasps of the crowd who **(8)** .... *(watch)* the flight. Santos-Dumont was elated when he realised he **(9)** .... *(win)*, but at first the officials **(10)** .... *(refuse)* to give him the prize. Although he **(11)** .... *(reach)* his destination in under thirty minutes, there **(12)** .... *(be)* a delay while his mooring line was secured. At some point the rules **(13)** .... *(change)* to make the official time of landing when a balloon's guide rope was caught from the ground – but Santos-Dumont maintained that he **(14)** .... *(never / tell)* this. A few days later, newspapers reported that the prize **(15)** .... *(award)* to Santos-Dumont in a time of 29 minutes and 30 seconds and he **(16)** .... *(become)* known all over the world as a pioneering aviator. After he **(17)** .... *(receive)* the prize money, Alberto **(18)** .... *(charm)* the people of Paris by giving some of the money to his crew and donating the rest to the poor people of the city.

> **Grammar tip**
>
> We can also use an *-ing* form with *after* instead of the past perfect or past simple when the subject is the same in both clauses, e.g. *After receiving the prize money, he charmed the people of Paris.*

✏️ EXAM TASK: Speaking (Part 2)

6 **Prepare answers to the questions. in pairs, take turns to talk about the topic for one to two minutes.**

Describe a decision you made in the past, e.g. to travel to a particular country or to change your job.

You should say:
    what the decision was
    why you made that decision
    what events or feelings led to your decision
and explain why this was a good or bad decision.

The future of schooling

1 **Work in pairs. Discuss the questions.**

a) What do you enjoy about learning English?   **b)** Do you use online materials to help you?

c) Why are you taking the IELTS exam?   **d)** What are you planning to do after taking the IELTS exam?

2a **Check your grammar!** **Read what these students say. Underline all the forms which the students use to express the future.**

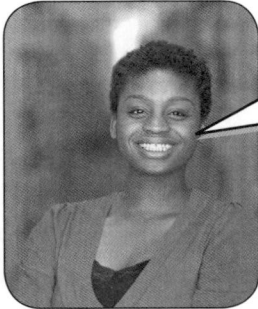

> I'm studying pharmacy. As part of the course, I'm going to do a placement with a pharmaceutical company. It starts in the summer.

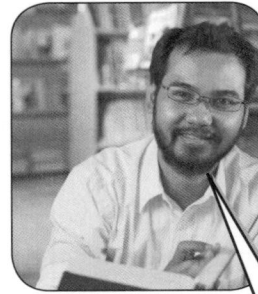

> I come to the library to study most days. When I finish my studies, I might take some time out to travel. I'm taking the IELTS exam next week. I hope my test score will improve my chances of getting a job in another country.

Grammar tip

In contexts where more than one future form can be used, the choice often depends on the speaker's perception of the future event. *Be going to* is often more informal than *will* and is rarely used in academic writing.

2b **How many different forms are used to talk about the future in exercise 2a? Which forms could be replaced with *be going to*? Would this change the meaning of the sentences?**

3a **Read the texts about education in the digital age and answer the questions.**

a) In text A, what questions are raised about the future of education?

b) In text B, what was Salman Khan's first job? What is he doing now?

A

EDUCATION IN THE DIGITAL AGE

While there is still a large digital divide between rich and poor nations, internet usage is rapidly increasing worldwide and according to Eric Schmidt, executive chairman of Google, we are on the verge of a truly global digital age. He predicts that by the end of the decade, the whole world will have learnt how to access information online. In the field of education this raises the inevitable question of how the digital competence of young people will affect classroom practice and equally how young students will navigate the vast amount of information that is available. Many consider that the role of a teacher is almost certain to change and is likely to become that of a mentor and facilitator.

B

Sal Khan, founder of the Khan Academy, has been astonished by the success of the educational videos his organisation produces. When the former financial analyst designed a video to help his cousin learn maths, <u>he had no idea where it would lead</u>. Now a million students use his videos every month and Khan is predicting that <u>the future classroom will be flipped</u>. By this he means that students will learn the theory at home via a video and come to school to participate in practical activities with their peers and the teacher. Khan already knows teachers who are using his video material in this way and it is feasible that <u>in ten or twenty years</u>, <u>all US students will be following a similar learning model</u>. Khan foresees that <u>in the same time period, technology will become</u> <u>essential for performing a number of common duties</u>, such as generating tests, and will therefore greatly increase the amount of valuable time a teacher spends with a student. The goals of the Khan Academy are therefore not just to make the most of technology to flip the classroom but also to humanise the classroom experience.

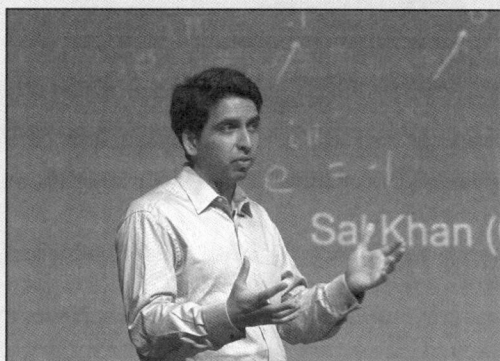

Sal Khan of the Khan Academy

3b Discuss in pairs. What predictions for the future of education are mentioned in the texts? Do you agree with them?

4 Read the Grammar reference. Choose examples for each point from the underlined phrases in the texts in exercise 3a. Add them to the Grammar reference.

Grammar tip

be (un)likely to or *be (almost) certain to* are useful ways to express degrees of probability in the future.

Grammar reference: future continuous and future perfect

- Use *will + be + -ing* (the future continuous) to talk about an action which will be in progress at a point in the future, e.g. **(1)** ....
- Use *will + have* + past participle (the future perfect) to predict that at a point in the future something has already happened. Time expressions *by …* or *before …* are common with the future perfect, e.g. **(2)** ....
  The continuous form of the future perfect (*will+ have been + -ing*) can also be used to place emphasis on the duration of the event, e.g. *This summer I will have been working as a teacher for ten years.*
- The verb *be* and state verbs generally take simple forms *(will be, will have been)*, e.g. **(3)** ....

Future in the past

- When you are talking about the past, use future forms in the past to talk about events which were in the future at that time, e.g. *He has no idea where it will lead.* > **(4)** ....
  Other future forms in the past are: *will > would; be + -ing > was / were+ -ing; be going to > was / were going to; be to > was / were to; be about to > was / were about to.*

Other future forms

- We can use the verb *be + to* + infinitive or *be + due to* + infinitive to talk about plans or arrangements, usually in a more formal context, e.g. *Sal Khan is to speak to delegates later this month.*
- *be about to, be on the verge / point of* are used to talk about events that will happen in the very near future, e.g. **(5)** ....
- Passive forms of the future simple, (*will + be* + past participle) and of the future perfect (*will + have been* + past participle), are used in academic writing, e.g. **(6)** ....

5 Read the text and choose the correct future form. Sometimes both forms are possible.

In 1999, Sugata Mitra was teaching people how to write computer programs in New Delhi. Next to where he worked was a slum. Mitra says, 'I used to think "How on Earth are those kids ever **(1)** *going to learn / learning* to write computer programs?" Mitra made a hole in the boundary wall of his office and placed a computer inside. He wanted to see what **(2)** *would / was going to* happen. Eight hours later, he found the children teaching each other how to browse the internet. Over the next 14 years, Mitra **(3)** *was to / was about to* place several hundred computers in learning stations across India and elsewhere in the 'Hole in the Wall' programme.

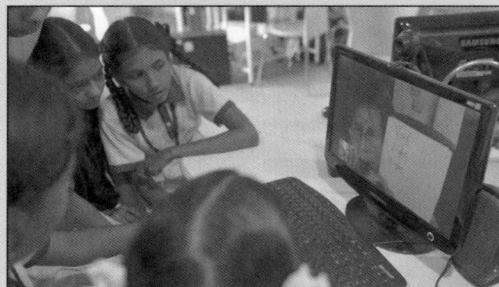

Students from Hyderabad, India, using the internet in class

Now Professor of Educational Technology at Newcastle University, Mitra has had his opinions of schooling radically changed by the project. Unlike some educators, Mitra does not believe that the education system **(4)** *is on the verge of / is about to* collapse. In Mitra's opinion, the system is outdated, and he promotes instead 'educational self-organisation' which allows learning to emerge. He even questions the idea of knowledge itself. 'Within five years, you **(5)** *will not be able to / will not have been able to* tell if somebody is consulting the internet or not. The internet **(6)** *will be / is due to be* inside our heads. […] What then will be the value of knowing things? We **(7)** *will / shall* have acquired a new sense. Knowing **(8)** *will have become / will have been becoming* collective.'

Mitra has developed the idea of a SOLE (Self-Organised Learning Environment) where children collaborate to find information. The results from a number of schools in India and the UK have been startling. However, Mitra admits the samples are small and **(9)** he *is to / is due to* conduct more rigorous measurements.

The lack of thorough academic findings troubles Mitra's critics. They are not convinced that in a number of years all students **(10)** *will be learning / will have been learning* in SOLEs and some critics see the experiment as a novelty which **(11)** *will have faded away / will be fading away* before many years have passed. However, as technology continues to change the world in which we live, and many educators worry that traditional skills and even human intelligence **(12)** *are going to replace / will be replaced* by technology, the questions Mitra is asking about the future of knowledge and learning are becoming increasingly pertinent.

6 Discuss in pairs. Do you agree with these statements about classrooms of the future? Amend the statements to reflect your opinions.

a) Technology is about to cause a revolution in the classroom.

b) Using more technology in the classroom will only be beneficial for some students.

c) In classrooms of the future, learning how to do maths sums will be irrelevant.

d) In ten years' time, our children will not be learning handwriting.

e) There will soon be no schools.

> **Grammar tip**
>
> *I shall / we shall* are used by some British people as an alternative to *I will / we will*. It is not common in academic writing. *Shall we / Shall I …?* are more often used to make suggestions or offers, e.g. *Shall we go?*

✎ EXAM TASK: Writing (Task 2)

7 Write about the topic below. Give reasons for your answer and include any relevant examples from your own knowledge or experience. Use different forms of the future in your answer.

> Computers in schools will never be able to replace the teacher.
>
> To what extent do you agree or disagree?

90 mins

Toxic footprint

1 **What do you think? Discuss the questions in pairs.**

a) Think of an item of clothing you own. How do you think it was made? Do you think chemicals were used in the production of this item of clothing?

b) Which of the stages in the production of a cotton garment – dyeing, washing or weaving – does this photo show? What do you think? Why might chemicals be used at this stage?

2 **Check your grammar!** **The diagrams below show the manufacturing process of the fabric rayon. Complete the sentences describing the process, using the verbs in the box to help you.**

> combine   dry   filter   look   shred   soak (x2)   store   turn into

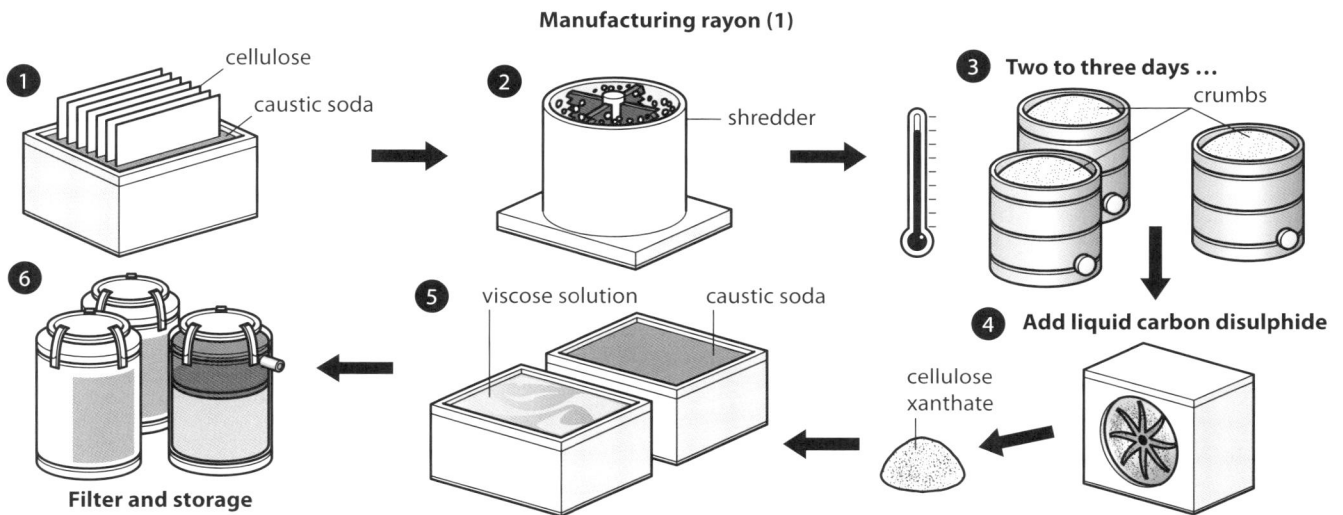

Manufacturing rayon (1)

- cellulose
- caustic soda
- 1
- 2 shredder
- 3 Two to three days ... crumbs
- 4 Add liquid carbon disulphide
- cellulose xanthate
- 5 viscose solution caustic soda
- 6 **Filter and storage**

1 To make rayon, sheets of cellulose (or wood pulp) .... in caustic soda.

2 The dried and pressed sheets .... into tiny pieces, which are called crumbs.

3 The crumbs .... in metal containers for two to three days.

4 The crumbs .... with liquid carbon disulphide, which .... them .... an orange substance called sodium cellulose xanthate.

5 The cellulose xanthate .... in caustic soda. The resulting viscose solution .... similar to honey.

6 The viscose solution .... for impurities and .... in vats for four to five days.

3 **Which word can be used in all the gaps in the sentences below?**

1 Use a .... structure to focus on an action or object instead of the person or thing that does the action, e.g. *(Workers store the crumbs in metal containers.)* > *The crumbs **are stored** in metal containers.*

2 The .... form of the verb is used when the person or thing that does the action (the agent) is obvious, not known or does not need to be mentioned, e.g. *Rayon **is made** from wood pulp.*

3 Present simple .... forms are often used in a description of a technical process, where the focus of attention is on the process.

4 .... structures are formed with a tense of the auxiliary *be* + past participle.

4 **Read about a further stage in the production process of rayon and label the diagram.**

The viscose solution is next turned into strings of fibres. This is done by forcing the liquid through a spinneret, which works like a shower-head, into an acid bath. After being bathed in acid, the fibres are ready to be spun into yarn. Depending on the type of yarn desired, several spinning methods could be used. In pot spinning, the fibres are first stretched onto a series of rollers called godet wheels. This stretching makes the fibres more uniform and also gives them more strength. The fibres are then put into a rapidly spinning cylinder called a Topham box, resulting in cake-like strings that stick to the sides of the box. The strings must then be washed, bleached, rinsed, dried and wound on cones or spools before being woven into fabric. The resulting fabric can be given any of a number of finishing treatments. These include fire, water or wrinkle resistance.

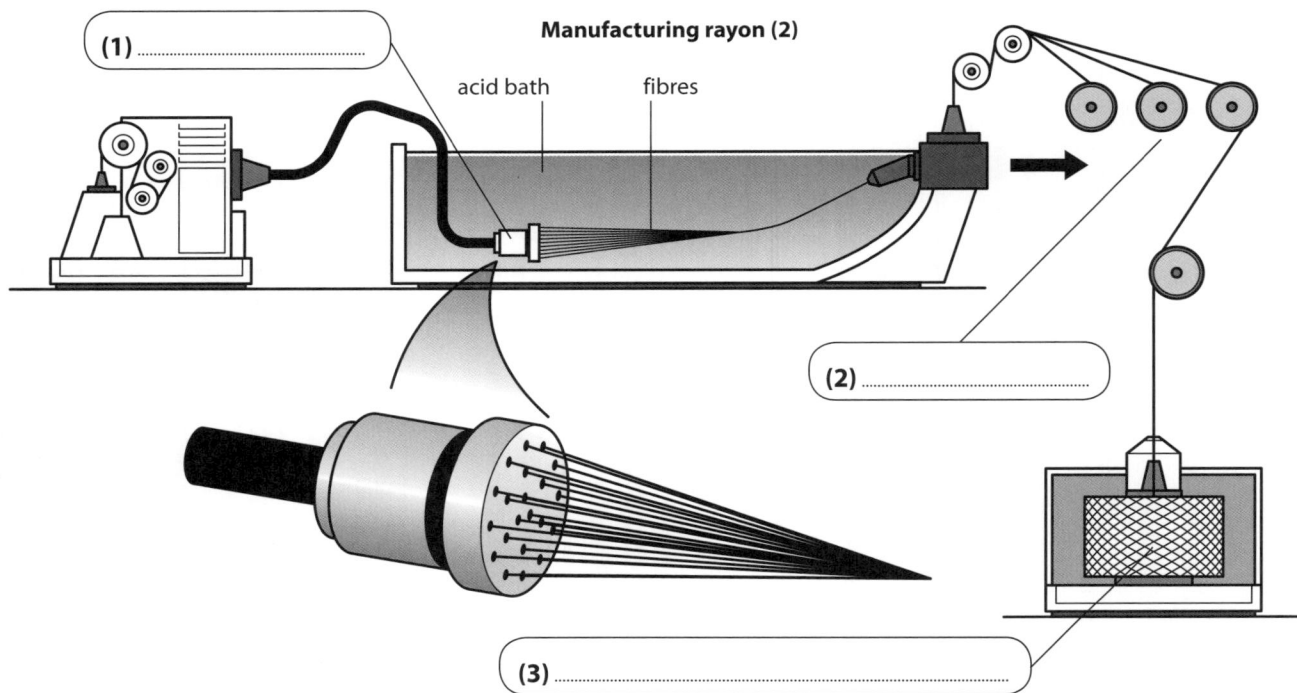

Manufacturing rayon (2)

(1) ....

acid bath   fibres

(2) ....

(3) ....

5 **Read the Grammar reference. Find examples of each point in the text in exercise 4 and add them to the Grammar reference.**

Grammar reference: passive forms

- Use a passive form after modals *can* and *could* to express possibility (+ *be* + past participle),
  e.g. **(1)** ....

- We can use a passive form after modal verbs of obligation, such as *must*, *should* and *had to*, (+ *be* + past participle), e.g. **(2)** ....

- In the passive, verb + infinitive or adjective + infinitive are followed by *to be* + past participle,
  e.g. **(3)** ....

- Verb + *-ing* form or preposition + *-ing* form are followed by *being* + past participle,
  e.g. **(4)** ....

- Passives are common in academic writing to report (not necessarily agree with) an opinion,
  e.g. *It is believed / claimed / said / thought / understood that … ; It has been argued / reported that … ;*
  … is/are (not) expected / known to … ; … is/are (not) considered to be … ; has/have (not) been found / shown to … .

6 Read the text about artificial silk and answer the questions, using the Grammar reference to help you.

a) What forms of the passive are used in sentences 1–3?

b) Look at sentence 1. How could you rewrite this sentence using an active form of the verb? What reasons might the writer have for choosing a passive construction instead?

c) In sentence 2, the writer chooses to start the sentence by referring back to the disease. Why do you think this is?

d) Find a way to rewrite sentence 5 which avoids repetition of 'Chardonnet' and doesn't use 'he'.

e) In sentence 6, the writer has used the verb 'appear'. Is there a passive form of the verb 'appear'? Rewrite the sentence using the verb 'develop'.

(1) In the 1860s the French silk industry was being threatened by a disease which affected the silkworm. (2) A solution to the disease was found by Louis Pasteur, who had already invented the process of pasteurisation, assisted by Count Hilaire de Chardonnet. (3) Chardonnet discovered by chance that artificial silk could be produced from cellulose. (4) He received his first patent for artificial silk in 1884. (5) Shortly after Chardonnet built his first factory. (6) Early artificial silk was highly flammable and more stable versions of the material (or rayon) subsequently appeared.

Hilaire de Chardonnet

Grammar tip

Using the passive allows a writer to change the order of information in a text. This is useful for greater clarity, e.g. putting longer expressions at the end of a clause, or greater readability, e.g. avoiding repeating the subject.

7 Combine the parts of the sentence using the correct active or passive form of the words in brackets.

a) The toxic footprint of textiles / a serious environmental and health issue. (*become*)

b) Both workers and consumers / by the chemicals that are used at each textile processing stage. (*risk / affect*)

c) Some finishing treatments, such as water resistance / to have hazardous properties. (*show*)

d) Consumers are likely / chemicals by inhaling fibre dust from a textile. (*expose to*)

e) Besides / a range of health issues, some chemicals from clothing accumulate in the environment. (*link to*)

f) The fashion industry / to have an enormous impact on the environment. (*seem*)

g) Manufacturers / chemicals on garment labels. (*not / expect / list*)

h) The Global Organic Textile Standard (GOTS) / one of the world's leading processing standards for textiles. (*consider / be*)

i) The GOTS logo / only on clothes which meet certain environmental standards. (*may / display*)

j) The chemicals in all the processing stages of a garment / environmental criteria. (*must / meet*)

✎ EXAM TASK: Speaking (Part 3)

8 Work in pairs. Discuss the questions.

Why is the textile industry a problem for the environment?

Do you think people are adequately aware of environmental issues in the textile industry?

What do you think governments could do to tackle the problem of our toxic footprint?

Infographics

1 Look at the infographic. Then cover the pictures and try to remember the information. Which parts of the information do you find easiest to remember? Why?

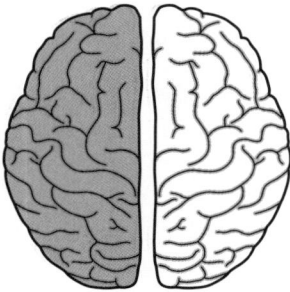

ALMOST
50%
of your brain is involved in
visual processing

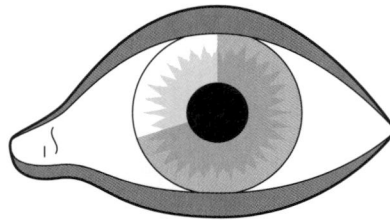

70%
of your sensory receptors are
in your eyes

1/10
OF A SECOND
is the time it takes for you to
understand a visual scene

2 Read the texts and answer the questions. (Don't complete the sentences at this stage.)

a) Why do people often like infographics?   **b)** Why have infographics become more popular recently?

What is an infographic?

An information graphic or **infographic** is any visual representation of data. Infographics are used to express a large **(1)** .... often complex information simply and clearly. The most common infographics are pie charts and graphs, but visual solutions are becoming ever more creative. Infographics are often used in education, journalism, economics and marketing. As technology feeds a global demand for knowledge, and with computers to analyse the facts, there has been a massive increase in data journalism and it is hard to find a newspaper or news site that does not have any infographics.

What is data?

Data is raw facts. **(2)** .... examples of data are words, numbers, dates, images and sounds. Data is processed by computers to become information. Information is a collection of data put into context.

Why infographics?

Infographics are accessible and easier to recall. Our brains have a high capacity for storing visuals in our long-term memory. We remember comparatively **(3)** .... the information we hear (10%) or read (20%), but as much as 80% of what we see and do.

(4) .... **information is too much?**
Research shows that our brains receive five times more information every day than thirty years ago. Visual content eases processing and provides some respite from the textual load that makes up **(5)** .... our daily browsing and **(6)** .... our work-related activities.

3 **Check your grammar!** Answer the questions, referring back to examples in the text to help you.

a) How many uncountable nouns can you find in the text?

b) What form of the verb do uncountable nouns usually take?

c) What forms of the verb can countable nouns take?

d) Can uncountable nouns end in -*s*?

4 **Compare the uses of the nouns in bold in these sentences. What do you notice?**

a) Infographics are often used in **education**.

b) Every child deserves the chance of an **education.**

5 **Complete the sentences in the texts in exercise 2 with the quantifiers in the word box, using the Grammar reference to help you. You may need to add *of*.**

amount   how much   little   many   much   some

Grammar tip

Some nouns can be countable or uncountable depending on their meaning. Uncountable nouns usually refer to a more general use and countable nouns to a more particular use. Some other examples are *content, experience, life, memory, technology, time.*

Grammar reference: quantifiers

Use with countable or uncountable nouns

The following words are all used in front of a noun to express quantity:

- *many, a few / few* and *several* are used with countable nouns
- *much, a little / little* are used with uncountable nouns
- *all, plenty of, a lot of / lots of, some, any, hardly any, no, none of* can be used with both countable and uncountable nouns

Use with *of*

- *plenty, a lot / lots* and *none* always take *of*, e.g. *plenty of information*
- Other quantifiers use *of* with a pronoun or if there is a determiner (e.g. *a, the, this, your*) before the noun, e.g. *several of them, much of your time.*
- *all* is common without *of* in front of determiner + noun, e.g. *all (of) the information*
- Many quantifiers (without *of*) can be used as pronouns, e.g. *Some say cave paintings were the first infographics.* (Note that *no* can't be used in this way.)

Meaning of quantifiers

- *a few / a little* have a neutral or positive meaning; *few / little* can be used with a negative meaning, e.g. *Few people realise the risks.* (= less than expected or hoped for)
- *no* means the same as *not any*; use *no* for greater emphasis or to start a sentence, e.g. *No newspaper article is complete without an infographic.* Use *none of* with a pronoun, e.g. *none of them,* or a determiner + noun, e.g. *none of the people.*
- *a number of* has a similar meaning to *some*; use *a (large) number of* with countable nouns or *an amount / a large amount of* with uncountable nouns to mean 'many' or 'much'. Alternatives are: *a considerable* or *significant number / amount, a large / good proportion* (of) or *a majority.* For smaller amounts use *a small fraction* (of) or a (*small*) *minority* (of).
- Use *enough* to mean 'sufficient'. Use *too much / too many* to mean 'more than is necessary or reasonable'.

6 **Work in pairs. Do you agree with these statements? Amend the statements to reflect your opinions.**

a) There is too much advertising on the internet.

b) No government money should be spent on athletics.

c) There is not enough time spent learning about technology in school.

d) Economics is a topic that appeals to a large number of people.

e) Many of the stories that headline on news sites are unimportant.

f) Technology takes up a large amount of our time.

7 **Look at the pie chart. Circle the correct quantifiers to complete the text.**

Chart showing the number of hours' sleep 100 students from Hervey College have during exams

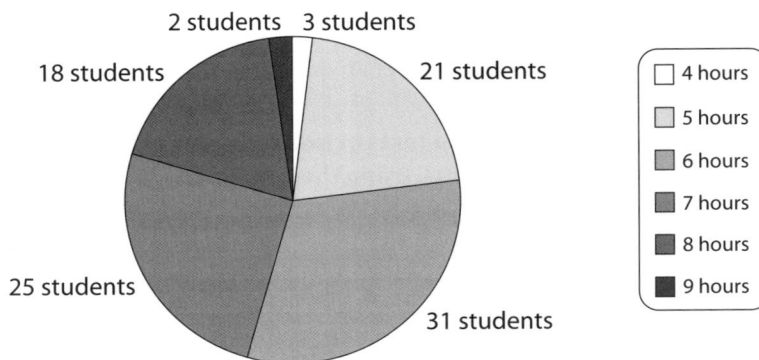

2 students 3 students
18 students 21 students
25 students
31 students

☐ 4 hours
☐ 5 hours
▨ 6 hours
▨ 7 hours
▨ 8 hours
■ 9 hours

While many people love pie charts, there are **(1)** *plenty of / some* who believe that pie charts are over-used. Edward Tufte, a pioneer in infographics, believes that 'the only thing worse than a pie chart is **(2)** *much / several* of them.' Pie charts are not appropriate for **(3)** *all / plenty* data we want to represent visually. Pie charts are best used when there are **(4)** *a few / a little* categories, usually no more than six, which show variation in size. If there are too **(5)** *much / many* similar-sized categories, a pie chart can be difficult to interpret.

In this example, the **(6)** *amount / number* of sleep students in Hervey College get during exams is represented in a pie chart. Users are able to draw both detailed and general conclusions from the chart at a glance. For example, the total number of people surveyed was 100. A **(7)** *some / number* of students (approximately a fifth) had eight hours sleep. **(8)** *No / None* of the students slept for more than nine hours. A quarter of the students managed seven hours' sleep during the exam period. A **(9)** *small fraction / significant proportion* of students (32%) had six hours' sleep. Around 20% of students reported having **(10)** *few / little* sleep (five hours), with **(11)** *a few / a little* only getting four hours. If the recommended average for a night's sleep is seven or eight hours, then approximately half of the students in this class did not get **(12)** *too much / enough* sleep during exam time.

✐ EXAM TASK: Writing (Task 1)

8a **The bar chart below represents the results of a survey to which there were 9,800 respondents. Summarise the information by selecting and reporting the main features. Use quantifiers where appropriate.**

Attendance at cultural events and visits to places of culture in Scotland in 2014

> **Grammar tip**
>
> Use *the number of* with a singular verb to talk about the size of a group, e.g. *The (total) number of people surveyed was 100.*

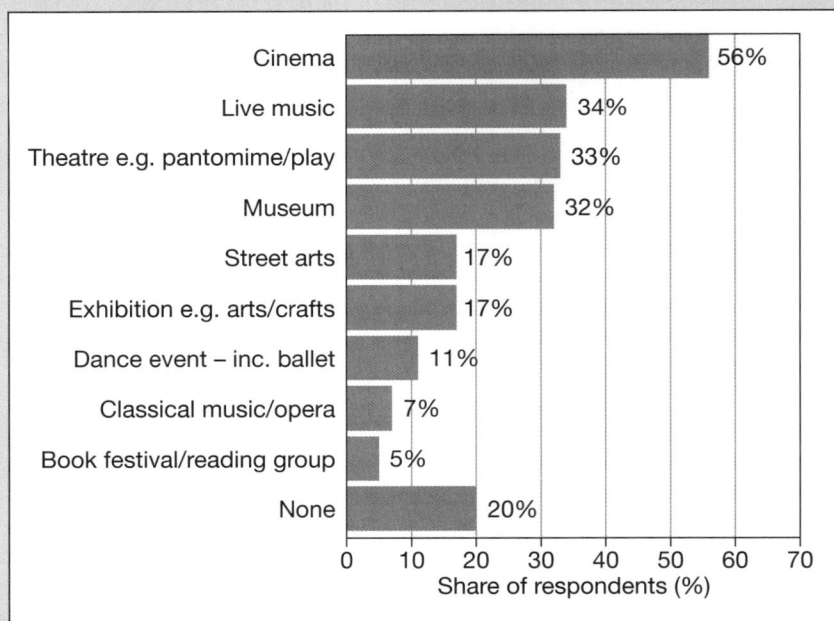

Cinema	56%
Live music	34%
Theatre e.g. pantomime/play	33%
Museum	32%
Street arts	17%
Exhibition e.g. arts/crafts	17%
Dance event – inc. ballet	11%
Classical music/opera	7%
Book festival/reading group	5%
None	20%

Share of respondents (%)

8b **Discuss in pairs. Why are bar charts useful? Which do you find easier to use, pie charts or bar charts?**

PHOTOCOPIABLE ⟋⟋⟋

Pictures of the floating world

1 Look at the two prints by the Japanese artist, Katsushika Hokusai. Which do you prefer and why?

2a **Check your grammar!** Read the texts describing the prints. One of the texts is missing some words. Which text is it? What kind of words are missing?

A In 1831, at peak of his long career, Hokusai produced series of woodblock prints, entitled *Rare Views of Japanese Bridges*. Series depicts scenes of <u>daily life</u> on and around bridges in Japan. In *Tenma Bridge in Setsu Province*, fleet of ships passes beneath curved bridge. <u>People</u> crowd <u>bridge</u> to watch <u>ships</u>.

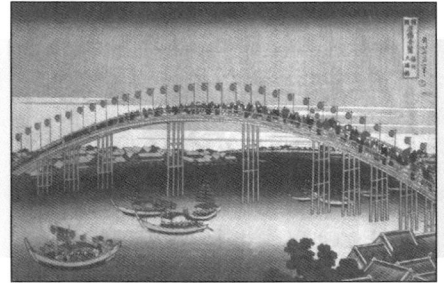

B Representations of <u>water</u> were a key subject for Japanese artists and Hokusai in particular. The woodblock print below is a well-known image depicting a large <u>whale</u> surrounded by tiny boats, as seen from a high point on the coast of the Goto islands in the East China Sea. Similar to a photograph, the frame of the image cuts off parts of the picture, like the tree that juts out over the water, but disappears from the audience's view.

2b Work in pairs to add the missing words. Check your answers in the key.

3 Look at the underlined words in the text. Find examples of single and plural countable nouns and uncountable nouns. Complete the table.

	a/ an	the	Ø (zero article)
Singular countable nouns	✔	✔	✘
Plural countable nouns			
Uncountable nouns			

Grammar tip

A singular countable noun is not used alone. We always use a determiner in front, e.g. *a, an, the, your, this, each.*

4a Read the text. Why was Hokusai's work popular with Impressionist painters?

<u>The world</u> was largely unaware of Japanese printmaking, but that all changed when trade between Japan and the West started in the 1850s. <u>Traders</u> protected their goods by wrapping them in discarded prints. <u>When the prints made their way to Europe</u>, they astonished artists and collectors. In 1867, Japanese prints, among them works by Hokusai, were displayed to audiences from the West for <u>the first time</u>, bringing about *Japonisme* – <u>a craze</u> for collecting Japanese art – which spread throughout <u>Europe</u> and to the USA. Hokusai had moved away from <u>the images of well-known characters which were featured in earlier Japanese prints</u>. Instead, his work focused on the daily life of Japanese people. <u>A print</u> often known as *The Great Wave* is probably the most famous of Hokusai's works and shows fishermen battling <u>the sea</u>.

The Japanese prints appealed to artists from the Impressionism movement, such as Claude Monet and Vincent Van Gogh. While <u>Western artists</u> tried to create the illusion of three-dimensional space, Japanese artists frequently showed flattened space in their work, using shapes like building blocks. This treatment of perspective, as well as the recurrent theme of <u>nature</u> and the interest in all levels of society, including <u>the poor</u>, reaffirmed some of the Impressionists' own artistic beliefs and inspired them to incorporate Japanese styles into their own work.

4b   **Read the Grammar reference. Choose examples for each point from the underlined phrases in the text in exercise 4a. Add them to the Grammar reference.**

Grammar reference: articles

Definite article

- Use the definite article (*the*) to refer to a definite thing the listener / reader knows about, or when it is clear from the context which thing you are referring to, e.g. *In 1831, Hokusai produced a series of prints. The series depicts … ; Traders protected their goods by wrapping them in discarded prints.* **(1)** ....
- Use *the* to refer to something specified or identified by the speaker / writer, e.g. *the woodblock print below,* **(2)** ....
- Use *the* to talk about things which are unique, this includes many examples of the environment around us, e.g. *the land, the rain,* **(3)** .... , **(4)** .... as well as the names of island and mountain groups, oceans and rivers, deserts, museums and hotels, e.g. *the Goto Islands, the East China Sea.*
- Ordinal numbers and superlative adjectives are usually preceded by *the*, e.g. *the most famous,* **(5)** ....

Indefinite article

- Use the indefinite article (*a* or *an*) to introduce one person, thing or topic into our conversation, e.g. *Whaling off Goto depicts a large whale;* **(6)** ....
- Use *a / an* to describe what someone / something is, e.g. *It is a well-known image. He was an artist.* **(7)** ....

No article

- Use no article to talk about things in general, e.g. *representations of water,* **(8)** .... , **(9)** .... Also with most (but not all) names of people, streets, towns, countries, continents, states etc., e.g. *Hokusai, Japan,* **(10)** ....
- We often use no article to generalise about the members of a group, e.g. *Impressionist painters, Japanese people, art lovers,* **(11)** .... , but use *the* to talk about a closed group of people, particularly if the group is well-known, e.g. *the Impressionists, the Japanese, the audience.* There are a number of expressions using *the* + adjective to describe a group, e.g. *the rich, the unemployed,* **(12)** .... We can use no article or *the* to refer to animal species, e.g. *Tigers are / The tiger is a powerful symbol in Japanese art.*

> **Grammar tip**
>
> Learn names of places and geographical features together with the article that goes with them, e.g. *Mount Fuji, the Alps, Japan, the USA.*

---

5   **Read the text and circle the best options.**

(1) *An / The* extensive collection of *ukiyo-e* can be seen in **(2)** *the / Ø* Tokyo National Museum. *Ukiyo-e* (pronounced yoo-kee-oh-ey) is the name for woodblock prints made during **(3)** *the / an* Edo period, which ended in **(4)** *the / Ø* 1868. *Ukiyo-e* translates as 'pictures of the floating world' and expresses both the Buddhist idea of the transitory nature of life and also a more hedonistic joy of the present. The single-sheet prints were mass-produced and sold by street vendors and shopkeepers, with **(5)** *a / the* single print costing as little as **(6)** *a / the* bowl of noodle soup.

(7) *A / The* print is a copy of an image, usually made on **(8)** *Ø / paper*. Printmakers made ink with **(9)** *the / Ø* natural pigments, which were powders made by grinding materials, such as **(10)** *the / Ø* flower petals. **(11)** *The / Ø* pigments produced a soft and subtle range of colours, but they were hard to make and faded quickly. Over time, **(12)** *the / Ø* blue skies and waters in the images transformed to dull yellow-brown and green.

In **(13)** *Ø / the* 1830s, limited trade with **(14)** *the / Ø* Dutch and **(15)** *the / Ø* Chinese brought a new pigment, called Prussian blue, to Japan from **(16)** *the / Ø* Europe. It allowed artists to create **(17)** *a / the* variety of rich and durable shades of blue. **(18)** *The / An* introduction of Prussian blue triggered what scholars call the Blue Revolution.

> **Grammar tip**
>
> Materials are usually uncountable, e.g. *It's made of paper.* However, there may be countable uses, e.g. *Would you like a paper?* (= a newspaper); *a piece of / a sheet of paper.*

✏ EXAM TASK: Writing (Task 1)

6 The diagrams below show the stages and tools used in the process of making a woodblock print in the traditional Japanese style. Summarise the information by selecting and reporting the main features. Take particular care with the use of articles.

1 Drawing and pasting the design

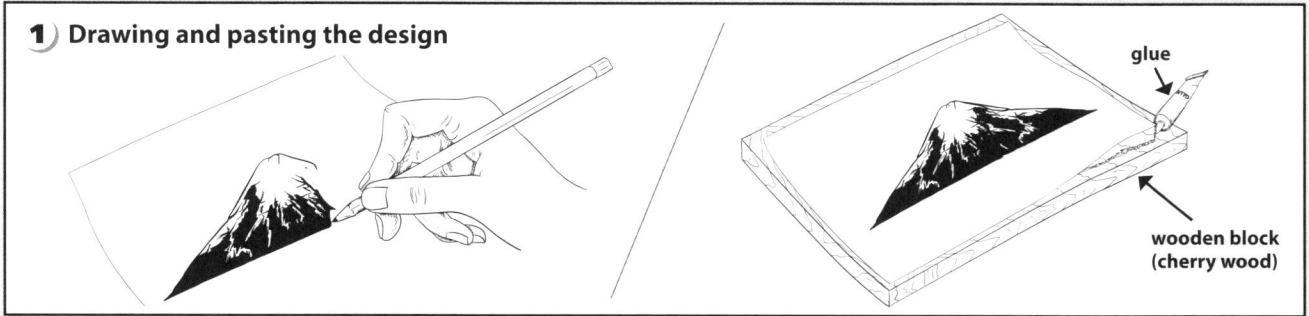

glue

wooden block (cherry wood)

2 Carving the key block

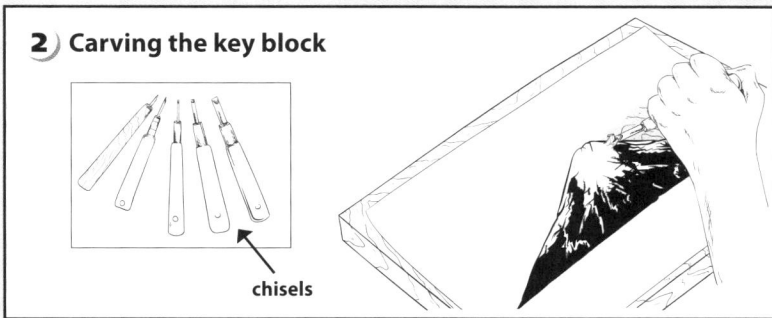

chisels

3 Applying the ink

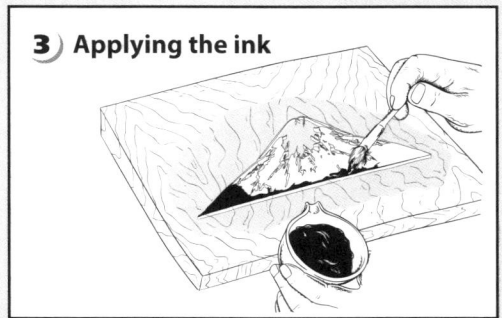

4 Pressing the ink on the paper

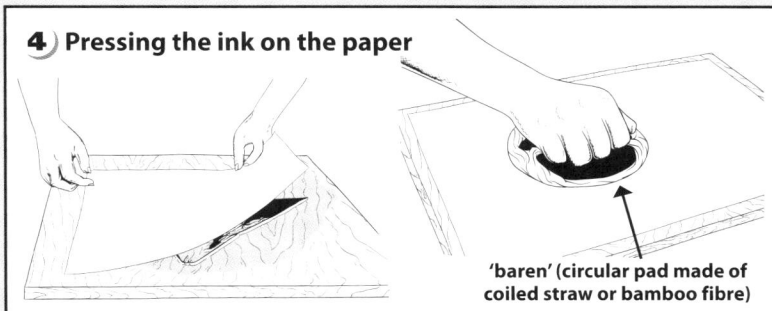

'baren' (circular pad made of coiled straw or bamboo fibre)

5 Printing

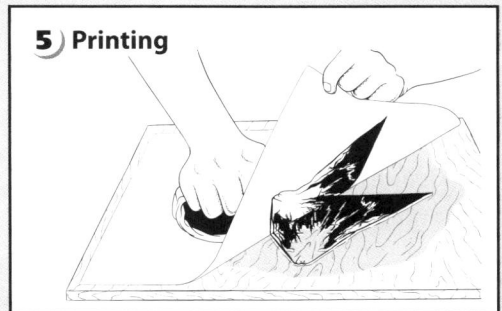

6 Drying and flattening

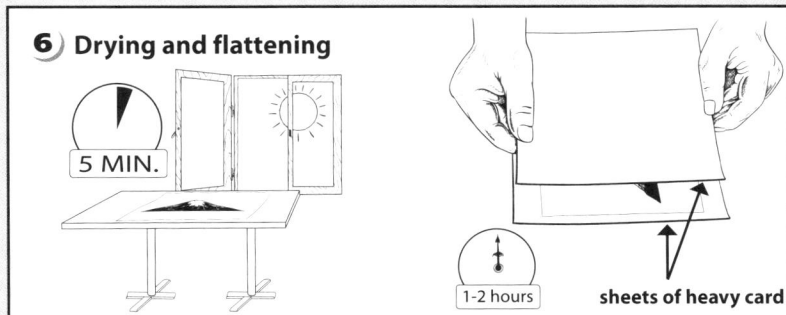

5 MIN.

1-2 hours

sheets of heavy card

7 The finished prints

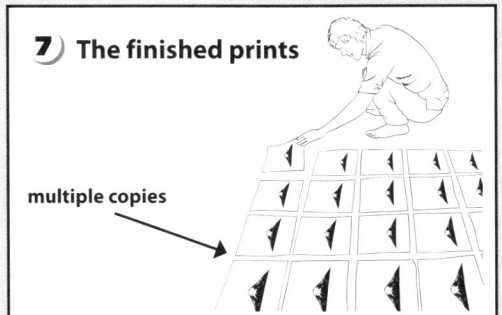

multiple copies

✏ EXAM TASK: Speaking (Part 3)

7 Work in pairs. Discuss the questions.

Do you enjoy art? Why / Why not?

In your country, what techniques and materials are traditional in art?

What benefits do painting or craftmaking have for people?

Selfish society

1a **Check your grammar!** Work in pairs. Complete the gaps in the quotes using the words from the box. Which of the words are pronouns?

> anything   every (x2)   no one   none   someone   we   yourself

1 .... should really love each other in peace and harmony.
Bob Marley

2 .... has ever become poor by giving.
Anne Frank

3 Friendship … is not something you learn in school. But if you haven't learned the meaning of friendship, you really haven't learned ....
Muhammad Ali

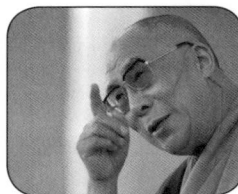

4 If you don't love ...., you cannot love others.
Dalai Lama

5 If you find it in your heart to care for .... else, you will have succeeded.
Maya Angelou

6 Do not fear mistakes. There are ....
Miles Davis

7 A pessimist sees the difficulty in .... opportunity; an optimist sees the opportunity in .... difficulty.
Winston Churchill

1b Discuss what each quote means. Which quote do you like best?

2 Read the Grammar reference. Which of the words in italics can be used in the sentences below?

Grammar reference: reflexive pronouns

- Use a reflexive pronoun as the object of the sentence when the subject and the object are the same, e.g. *If **you** do not love **yourself**, you cannot love others.*
- We can also use a reflexive pronoun after a preposition if the meaning is not clear otherwise, e.g. *Lucy was angry with **herself** for being late.*

a) We should really love *each other / one another / ourselves* in peace and harmony.

b) An optimist sees the opportunity in *every / each / all / both* difficulty.

c) Do not fear mistakes. There are *none / neither / not any*.

d) *No one / Nobody* has ever become poor by giving.

e) Tom should take better care of *him / himself*.

3a **Match the sentence beginnings 1–9 with their endings a–i.**

1 Respect for <u>everyone else</u> is a quality

2 <u>None of us</u> shares content online out of generosity,

3 Technology affects <u>every aspect</u> of our lives,

4 As a result of social media <u>anyone</u> has the chance to

5 It is important for <u>someone</u>

6 The power of technology is <u>something to celebrate</u>,

7 Everyone should also ask <u>themselves whether</u>

8 Consider <u>all the bloggers</u> and members of internet forums

9 Facebook™ and Twitter™ are the most popular social media platforms and <u>both</u>

a) who give freely of their time and advice.

b) not something to mistrust.

c) they are sometimes not selfish enough.

d) to take care of themselves if they want to take care of others.

e) lacking in society today, despite the fact that we are hyper-connected.

f) in fact we are just promoting ourselves.

g) including the ways we interact with others.

h) are thought to encourage selfish behaviour.

i) engage in issues which they care about.

3b **Discuss in pairs. Which sentences do you agree with?**

4 **Read the Grammar reference. Match the underlined words in the sentences above with the descriptions a–i in the Grammar reference.**

> **Grammar tip**
>
> *everybody vs. everyone*: indefinite pronouns ending in *-one* are more common in writing.

Grammar reference: determiners and indefinite pronouns

Determiners

- Determiners are used in front of a noun. The determiners *each* and *every, either* or *neither* are used with single countable nouns. Use *both* with plural countable nouns and *all* with countable or uncountable nouns, e.g. *each person, both people, at all times, all technology.* **a)** ....

- *both, each, either* and *neither* can be used as pronouns, e.g. *There are two opinions, but I don't agree with either.* **b)** ....

- Use *all, both, each, either, neither, none* + *of* in front of personal pronouns and noun phrases, e.g. *both of them, none of the people here; all / both* + *of* take a plural form of the verb. A singular form of the verb is usual with *either / neither / none* + *of* in formal English. **c)** ....

- *all* is common without *of*, e.g. *all (of) the people here* **d)** ....

Indefinite pronouns, e.g. *nobody, someone, anyone, everything*

- We can use an adjective or infinitive after an indefinite pronoun, e.g. *someone special, something to dream of.* **e)** ....

- We can add *else* after indefinite pronouns to mean 'other', e.g. *I can't eat anything else. Can I speak to someone else?* **f)** ....

- Pronouns beginning with *some-* are common in affirmative sentences; pronouns with *any-* are used in questions and negatives. **g)** ....

- We can also use pronouns with *any-* to mean 'all' or 'it doesn't matter which' in affirmative sentences, e.g. *It's advice that anyone can follow.* **h)** ....

- Use *they / their / them / themselves* to refer back to indefinite pronouns, e.g. *Technology allows **everyone** to access information **they** would otherwise not be able to obtain. They* etc can also be used if you don't want to specify 'he' or 'she', e.g. *Online **a student** has a whole range of online courses available to **them**.* **i)** ....

✏ EXAM TASK: Writing (Task 2)

5 **Read the writing exam task. Discuss in pairs whether you agree or disagree with the statement. Which sentences from exercise 3a would you include in this task?**

> Technology is creating a selfish society, particularly amongst younger people.
>
> To what extent do you agree or disagree?
>
> Give reasons for your answer and include any relevant examples from your own knowledge or experience.

6 **Read the sample answer to the writing task in exercise 5. Circle the correct options.**

Due to the huge increase in social media use, we are creating a society where self-image and status are becoming increasingly important. However, this does not necessarily mean that as a society we have stopped supporting **(1)** themselves / each other.

On the one hand, some people argue that our obsession with social media means we ignore those near to us who are in need. Today **(2)** everyone / all of us is able to stay connected with others. However, social media platforms encourage us to be 'friends' with people who have similar interests and **(3)** none / neither *of these* friendships replaces being part of a community. Someone can be up-to-date on the social life of **(4)** no one / anyone famous and yet be ignorant about what is happening in **(5)** his / their local community.

However, it is easy to dismiss people – especially 18–30 year olds – as individualistic and to claim that, as a result of their interest in activities such as posting 'selfies', they are only capable of loving **(6)** themselves / them. A recent survey in the US by research group Achieve asked more than 2,500 young people if they regularly gave charitable donations or volunteered – **(7)** either / both activity demonstrates a strong sense of social engagement. 84% of **(8)** all / each the young people who responded had made a donation and 70% gave up an hour of their time each week. Many used social media to promote a good cause and considered they were doing **(9)** something useful / useful *something* to help.

7 **Work in pairs. Plan and write a conclusion to the sample essay in exercise 6. Include *each other, all of us* and *something* in your conclusion.**

Global learning

1 Read the article about some recent research into reading. Discuss in pairs. What do you think of the conclusions of the study? Can you think of any reasons for these findings?

Reading helps with your maths!

(1) .... may seem surprising that reading for pleasure could help to improve children's maths' scores. Yet researchers at the Institute of Education at London University have come to **(2)** .... in a recent study. The study analysed the results of tests taken at the age of sixteen by 6,000 children born in the same week in 1970. **(3)** ....

appears to indicate that reading for pleasure was an important factor in the children's development. The research found there was a 14.4% advantage in vocabulary, a 9.9% advantage in maths and an 8.6% advantage in spelling amongst children who read regularly from an early age, once their parents' educational background and own reading habits were taken into account.

(4) .... have been published at a time when there are continuing concerns that reading for pleasure amongst young people has declined.

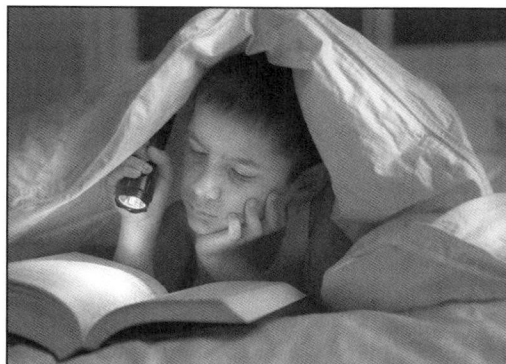

---

2 **Check your grammar!** Look at the article in exercise 1 again. What words do you think were used to complete the original article?

3a Read some further conclusions from the author of the study. Are any of these ideas similar to the ones you discussed in exercise 1?

It is widely accepted that reading for pleasure improves a child's vocabulary. However, Dr Alice Sullivan, the author of the recent study at London University, suggests, 'It is likely that a strong reading ability enables children to absorb and understand new information and affects their attainment in all subjects. According to Dr Sullivan, 'it is important to encourage a child's desire to read independently as it may promote a more self-sufficient approach to learning in general. In the survey, children who had read often at the age of ten and had been reading books and newspapers more than once a week aged sixteen had performed better in cognitive tests than those who had read less. These findings show it is essential for government policies to support and encourage children's reading, particularly in their teenage years.

There seems to be a tendency for today's young people to read less in their spare time than in previous generations. This is particularly worrying in the light of Dr Sullivan's research, which shows that reading less is likely to affect teenagers' intellectual development. Reading for pleasure tends to decline in secondary school so it is clear how crucial it is to provide access to a wide range of books in schools and libraries and to help young people discover authors they will enjoy.

Some people are concerned that the decline in reading for pleasure is the result of time spent online. However, that argument does not take into account the fact that e-readers and other new technologies make it easier to access books and newspapers.
Indeed in some countries where limited access to text has been a barrier to literacy, there is thought to be a link between improving literacy levels and the availability of mobile devices.

Grammar tip

that and *those* can be used to mean 'the one' and 'the ones'. In this text, *those who* = 'the ones / the children who'.

3b Read the Grammar reference. Choose examples for each point from the underlined parts of the text in exercise 3a and add them to the Grammar reference.

Grammar reference: *it* and *there* as preparatory subject

- Use *it* to start a sentence instead of a *to*-infinitive,
  e.g. **(1)** ....
  . (*it* + *be* + adjective / noun (+ *for* someone / something) + *to*-infinitive). This is more usual or natural than *To encourage a child's desire to read independently is important*. Note that this pattern is not used after *likely*, e.g. *They are likely to find a book there*. ~~It is likely for them to find a book there.~~

- We often use *it* instead of starting a sentence with a *that*-clause or question-word clause,
  e.g. **(2)** ....
  or **(3)** ....

- In academic writing, *it* as a preparatory subject is common with passive structures. This is useful when presenting a balanced argument as it allows you to distance your opinion from statements and claims, e.g. *It is widely accepted that … , It must be remembered that …* . Some other verbs commonly used in this way are: *believe, claim, demonstrate*, discover*, estimate, find, know, say, show*, suggest, think, understand*. (*These verbs are more commonly used in the past simple or present perfect.)

- *There* is used as a preparatory subject (*there is / are / was / were* + past participle + *to be / to have been*) with some reporting verbs, such as *believe, expect, report, say, think, understand*,
  e.g. **(4)** ....

- *It* and *there* can both be used with *seem / appear*, e.g. *It appears to indicate … / It appears that … , There seems to be,*
  (5) ....

Referring back using *it, this / these, that / those*

- We can use *it* and *this / that* to refer back to ideas or topics as well as single nouns that have already been mentioned in the text. Use *it* to continue referring to a topic that has already been established, e.g. *A child's desire to read independently is to be encouraged as **it** may promote a more self-sufficient approach to learning in general.* (*it* = a child's desire to read independently) Use *this* for greater emphasis or a new topic, e.g. *There seems to be a tendency for today's young people to read less in their spare time than in previous generations. **This** is particularly worrying because …*

- We often use *this / these* + noun phrase to summarise an idea that has been previously expressed,
  e.g. **(6)** ....

- *That* and *those* can imply a greater distance from the writer in time, such as in phrases used to refer to the past, e.g. *at that time / in those days; that* can also be used to distance oneself from the opinion of another person,
  e.g. **(7)** ....

4 Rewrite the paragraphs. Include the words given in brackets at the points in the sentences marked with an asterisk (*). Do not change the words given. Use any additional words necessary.

a) **(1)** *a fifth of all children in England, and close to a third of disadvantaged children, are unable to read well when they leave primary school. *(completely unacceptable)* **(2)** * creates obstacles to a fairer society. *(situation)* **(3)** It is not just impossible * experience the joy of reading. *(for these children)* **(4)** * prevent poorer children from achieving their potential in secondary school and beyond. *(also more likely)*

b) **(1)** * over 750 million adults worldwide who are illiterate. *(are believed)* **(2)** Roughly two-thirds * are female. *(cannot read or write)* **(3)** * population growth has caused this global literacy crisis. *(often claimed)* **(4)** However, * underinvestment in adult literacy programmes in many communities and workplaces is also to blame. *(probable)*

c) **(1)** Of the 650 million primary school age children in the world, * 250 million are not learning basic literacy skills. *(thought)* **(2)** However, * remembered that tremendous progress has been made in some countries. *(must)* **(3)** An estimated 17 million more children are now learning the basics at school in sub-Saharan Africa – * due in part to the abolition of school fees. *(this)* **(4)** * represents an impressive 45% more children learning at schools. *(figure)*

d) **(1)** It is becoming more and more evident *mobile technology could be for literacy development *(important)*. **(2)** *Hundreds of thousands of people in countries like Ethiopia, Nigeria and Pakistan are reading more now that they can read on their mobile phones. *(seems)* **(3)** A survey conducted by UNESCO reveals that * was more pronounced among women than men. *(trend)* **(4)** *One in three mobile readers are reading to their children from their phones. *(also significant)* **(5)** *high-light the potential of mobile technology for literacy programmes. *(examples)*

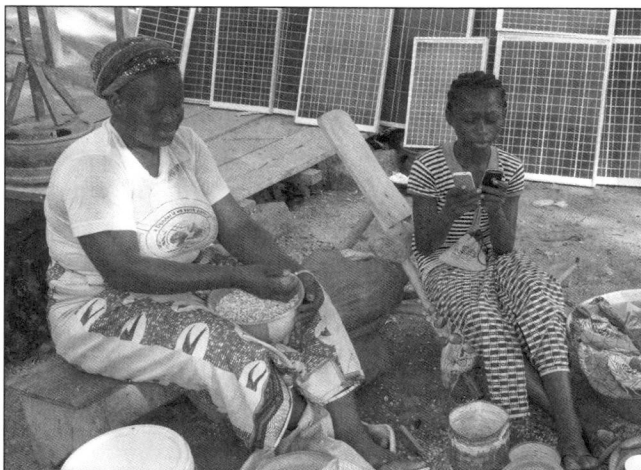

Grammar reference: preparatory *it* as object

We can sometimes use preparatory *it* as an object. Some common patterns are:

- *(dis)like, enjoy, love, hate, can't stand, prefer + it + if*-clause / question-word clause, e.g. *I enjoy it when the teacher reads to us.*
- *consider / find + it* + adjective + *to*-infinitive / *that*-clause / question-word clause, e.g. *I find it unacceptable that …*

✏ EXAM TASK: Speaking (Part 3)

5   **Work in pairs. Discuss the questions. Use some of the phrases in the Grammar reference above in your discussion.**

> How much time do you have for reading? When or where do you find it easiest or most difficult to read?
>
> Do you like it when favourite books are adapted into films?
>
> Do you think literacy levels worldwide are acceptable? Why? / Why not?

✏ EXAM TASK: Writing (Task 2)

6   **Write about the topic below. Give reasons for your answer and include any relevant examples from your own knowledge or experience. Use different structures that you have looked at in this lesson. Underline the examples you use in your answer and compare in pairs.**

> Some people say that reading is something which parents should encourage in children at home. Others, however, believe governments and schools have a responsibility to motivate students to read more.
>
> Discuss both these views and give your own opinion.

A more nutritious snack

1a Work in pairs. Look at the photos. What do you think is the connection between them? Skim read the text below and see if your ideas are similar.

A CONVERSATION STARTER

Eating insects may not be everyone's idea of fun, yet around 30% of the world's population eat bugs as part of their traditional diet and research shows that insects may contain **(1)** .... levels of protein than conventional meat. Nothing is **(2)** .... to get your dinner guests talking than the opportunity to sample deep-fried or chocolate-covered bugs – their presence on the menu is a great conversation starter – but there are other ways for your guests to try insects if they don't feel **(3)** .... as that. Insects ground into flour may be **(4)** .... for them to swallow than insects with whole legs and wings.

A food source in many different countries, crickets are probably **(5)** .... of all the edible bugs and they can be incorporated into your diet **(6)** .... than you'd think. Transform chocolate chip cookies into chocolate chirp cookies – a **(7)** .... and more nutritious snack – by using both plain flour and cricket flour and chopped dried crickets dipped in chocolate.

1b   **Check your grammar!** Complete the sentences in the text with comparative or superlative forms of the words in the box.

> adventurous   easily   hard   healthy   high   likely   well-known

2 Scientists are conducting research into edible bugs. Why do you think this is? Read the text from a science journal on page 35 and decide if the statements below are true or false.

a) Livestock farming takes up considerably less space than insect farming.

b) Farming methods for insects are much more environmentally-friendly than for conventional livestock.

c) All insects have a much higher nutritional value than meat.

d) Iron levels in honeybee larvae are the lowest out of all of the samples tested.

e) Calcium levels in insects are generally higher than in meat.

f) Insect foods have no potential disadvantages.

Grammar tip

Use one of these ways to describe progressive change:
more and more *difficult*
*hard**er** and hard**er***
increasingly *apparent* (more formal)

As the world population continues to rise, one of the largest challenges is securing global food supplies. In a number of countries, bugs such as silkworms, termites and crickets are traditionally collected when other food sources are in short supply. Grazing land for meat is becoming more and more difficult to find and scientists are looking for alternative sources of protein which can be produced on a viable commercial scale. According to current research, insects can be farmed **far more sustainably** than conventional livestock because they reproduce at an **even quicker** rate and are **significantly less demanding** in terms of living space. They also do not produce so many greenhouse gases.

A recent report compares the nutritional content of several commercially available insect species with three more commonly consumed forms of protein (chicken, pork and beef) and found that insects had nutritional values that were **just as high**. Indeed the nutritional values of beef and chicken were **considerably lower than** at least three insects. In general, meat contained less calcium, and analysis of iron content showed that the levels in honeybee larvae were **by far the highest** of all the protein sources tested. In addition to the economic and environmental benefits of raising insects, which are becoming increasingly apparent, these results suggest that insects may be good foods to promote in areas where food insecurity and malnutrition are major problems.

On a more cautionary note, the figures also showed that some insect foods had a **much higher** content of sodium and saturated fat than conventional livestock. This suggested that insect foods would be **slightly less suitable** to put forward as alternatives to meat in countries where there are a number of diseases linked to over-nutrition.

3a **Look at the comparative and superlative forms in bold in the text. Answer the questions.**

a) Which words are used to modify comparative forms? How about superlatives?

b) Which modifiers suggest a strong degree of difference?

3b **Compare your answers with the information in the Grammar reference.**

Grammar reference: modifying comparative and superlative forms

- Use words like *far* and *(very) much* to modify comparative forms of adjectives and adverbs. Other examples are *considerably* and *significantly*; *even* implies the difference is surprising. Use *a little, slightly, marginally* to indicate a smaller degree of difference.

- Words we can use to intensify superlatives include *much, by far, easily, quite (= absolutely)*; *one of, almost, nearly* and *probably* are common with superlatives too.

- Use *(not) so / as* + adjective + *as* to express similarity. We can use modifiers such as *(not) quite, (not) nearly, almost, just*. Alternatives are: *similar to, (approximately) equal to, (about) the same as* (less formal).

- To talk about quantity, use as *much / many* (+ noun) *as*. We can give more detail with words like *(more than) twice, (less than) half, three times*, e.g. *three times as much*.

- *more, fewer* and *less* are used in front of a noun; the superlative forms are *the most, the fewest* and *the least*.

4 Look at the chart showing relative amounts of greenhouse gases (GHGs) produced by different types of farming and complete the sentences using the words in brackets.

a) Beef cattle farming produces .... GHGs .... pig farming. *(twice)*

b) Insect farming produces .... GHGs .... livestock farming. *(far)*

c) GHG emissions from locusts are .... those from crickets. *(marginally)*

d) GHG emissions from mealworms are .... crickets. *(similar)*

e) .... GHG emissions come from beef cattle farming. *(easily)*

locust   mealworm

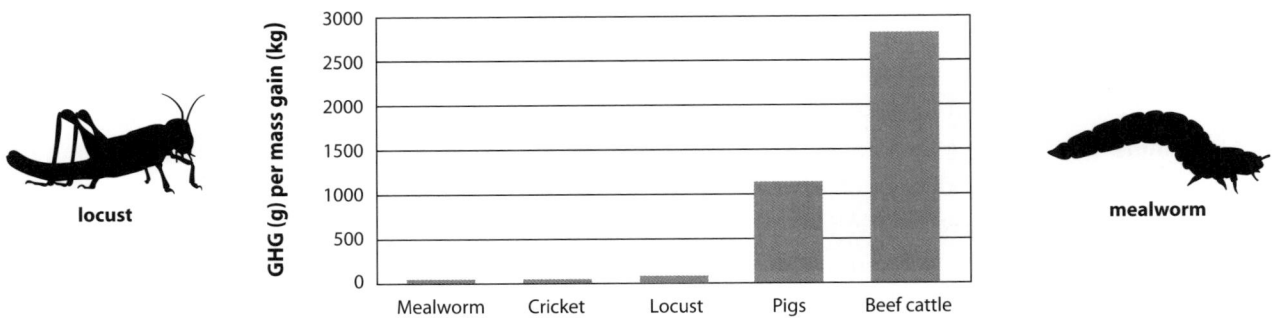

5a Look at the table and read the description. What is X?

Level (based on a 100g sample):

	Protein (g)	Calcium (mg)	Iron (mg)	Sodium (mg) = salt
Beef	20.6	5	1.95	60
Silkworm	14.8	42	1.8	14
Cricket (adult)	20.1	104	5.46	152

The level of X in crickets is by far the highest, and is more than twice as much as in a silkworm. X content in silkworms is much higher than in beef.

5b Discuss in pairs. Look at the table and compare the nutritional content of the food sources. On balance, which do you think is the most nutritious food source? Why?

✏ EXAM TASK: Writing (Task 1)

6 The charts below assess the environmental impacts associated with the farming of different protein-rich products. Summarise the information by selecting and reporting the main features, and make comparisons where relevant.

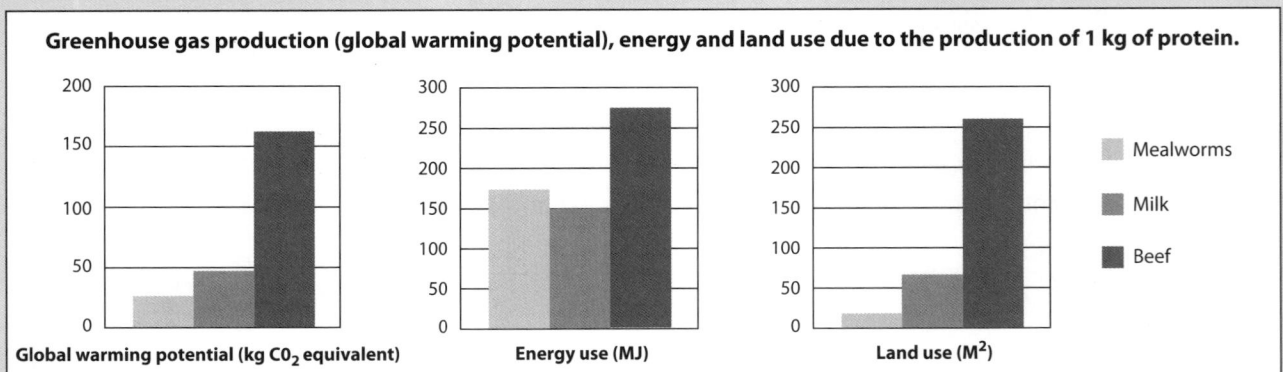

Greenhouse gas production (global warming potential), energy and land use due to the production of 1 kg of protein.

Global warming potential (kg CO_2 equivalent)

Energy use (MJ)

Land use (M^2)

Mealworms
Milk
Beef

The habit loop

1   Read the passage about habits and the brain and complete the diagram. Use no more than three words from the text.

The **(1)** .... enables us to make **(2)** ....

A behaviour is converted into

(3) .... in the

(4) ....

Scientific research into how our brains work could help people who <u>wish</u> to make long-lasting changes to their habits and routines. Learning a new skill takes a lot of effort. The mental energy required by <u>learning</u> to drive, for example, leaves many first-time drivers exhausted. Some even <u>consider</u> giving up. However, once a driver is accustomed to the new behaviour, it becomes automatic. An experienced motorist <u>can</u> drive while focussing on something else, such as listening to the radio or talking to passengers.

Developments in our understanding of the brain have <u>enabled</u> neuroscientists to trace our habit-making behaviours back to a part of the central brain called the basal ganglia, which also plays a key role in the development of emotions and memories. A part of the front brain, the prefrontal cortex, <u>allows</u> us to pay attention and make decisions. But as soon as our behaviour becomes automatic, the decision-making part of the brain <u>appears</u> to go into a state similar to a sleep mode. The capacity of our basal ganglia to take a behaviour and turn it into an automatic routine, <u>lets</u> us devote mental activity to something else.

2   **Check your grammar!** When you use two verbs together, the second verb may take a number of different forms. Write the underlined verbs from the text in the correct places on the mind map on page 38. One has been done as an example.

3 Work in pairs. Add the verbs to the mind map. Look up any you are not sure how to use in a dictionary.

> attempt   avoid   claim   could   deny   encourage   enjoy   hope   involve
> make   manage   must   permit   practise   remind   risk   warn

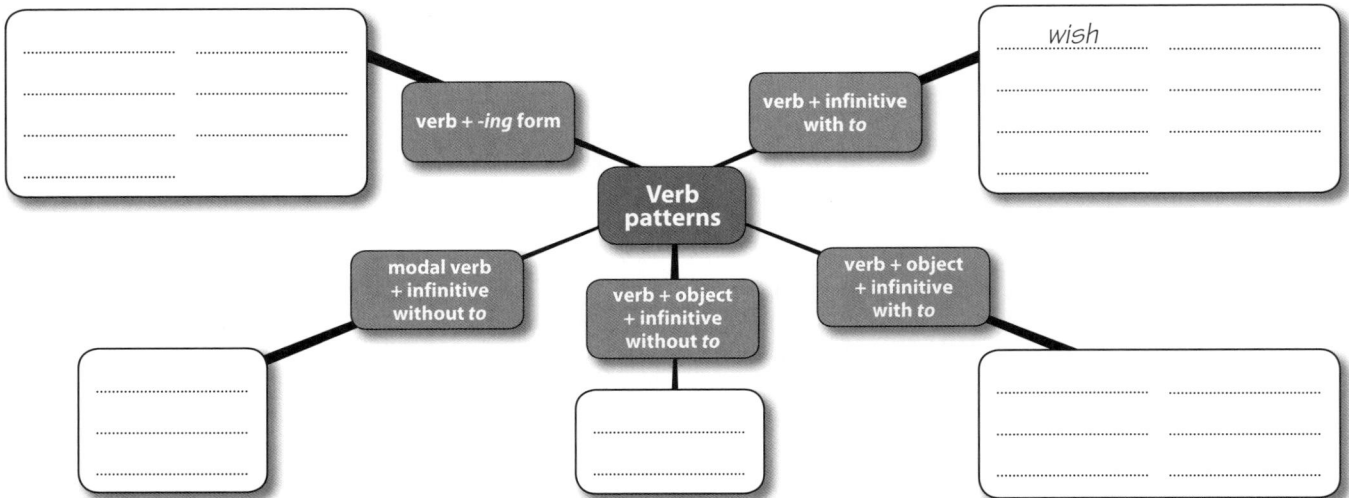

verb + -ing form

verb + infinitive with to

wish

Verb patterns

modal verb + infinitive without to

verb + object + infinitive without to

verb + object + infinitive with to

4 Circle the correct verb patterns in this text about the habit loop, using the information in the mind map to help you.

Therapists do not **(1)** claim _be able_ / _to be able_ to change all ingrained habits, but understanding a cycle known as the habit loop **(2)** can _ease_ / _to ease_ the process. Every habit consists of three components: a cue (or a trigger for an automatic behaviour to start), a routine (the behaviour itself) and a reward (which is how our brain **(3)** learns _to remember_ / _remembering_ this pattern for the future).

For people **(4)** hoping _to quit_ / _quitting_ a habit such as smoking, the process first **(5)** involves _to diagnose_ / _diagnosing_ their habit loop. This **(6)** enables individuals _find out_ / _to find out_ what factors trigger the habit. This knowledge is essential before **(7)** considering _to make_ / _making_ changes and a significant step in **(8)** letting people _feel_ / _to feel_ that they are regaining control. Therapists then **(9)** encourage patients _to follow_ / _following_ the golden rule of habit change which suggests that the most effective way to change a habit is to retain the old cue and reward and **(10)** attempt _to change_ / _changing_ only the routine.

5 Read the Grammar reference. Then complete the text on page 39, using the correct forms of the verbs in the word box.

Grammar reference: verb patterns

Verb + infinitive with _to_ or verb + _–ing_ form

Some verbs are followed by infinitive with _to_ or -ing form with no change in meaning, e.g. _start, begin, continue, like, love, hate, prefer_. For a few verbs (e.g. _remember, forget, regret, stop, go on, mean, need, try_) the choice of form depends on the meaning. Examples:

- _I stopped smoking when I was 30._ (stop + -ing form = not continue) _I stopped to ask the way._ (stop + infinitive with _to_ = pause in order to do something)

- _We went on working until the early hours._ (go on + -ing form = continue) _After working at the company for a few years, she went on to become the manager._ (go on + infinitive with _to_ = to do something after you have finished doing something else)

- _If you want to cut down on sugar, try not having it in your coffee._ (try + -ing form = discover if something works) _I know you're worried but try to get a good night's sleep._ (try + infinitive with _to_ = attempt to do something even if it does not work)

Verb + *that*-clause

Some verbs are commonly followed by a *that*-clause, e.g. *accept, acknowledge, admit, agree, believe, confirm, consider, decide, demand, deny, discover, doubt, ensure, estimate, expect, explain, hope, imply, learn, mean, note, notice, pretend, promise, realise, recommend, reveal, say, show, state, suggest, understand, wish.*

● Use *appear* or *seem* in the structure *it + that*-clause, e.g. *It appears that the prefrontal cortex can go into a sleep-like state.*

Grammar tip

Use *feel, hear, notice, see, watch* + object + infinitive without *to* for completed actions or + object + *-ing* form for actions in progress. Compare: *I **saw** the dog **bite** the cyclist. I **saw** her walk**ing** home.*

---

acknowledge	appear	bite	deny	make	notice	repeat	use	walk

Therapists do not **(1)** .... that habits are notoriously difficult to change. It requires much less effort to go on **(2)** .... a habit. Once an individual has **(3)** .... that they need to make changes, the next stage is to observe the cue for the behaviour. Someone who wants to stop **(4)** .... their nails, for example, may **(5)** .... themselves chewing their nails whenever they are bored. By replacing the routine with a different way to achieve relief from boredom – they could try **(6)** .... worry beads (a string of beads that can be manipulated with your hands) or **(7)** .... to a different room – an individual achieves the same reward. In this way, the cues and rewards stay the same, but the routine changes. By following this method, an individual can go on **(8)** .... a big difference to his or her life. Although some regression is inevitable, it **(9)** .... that in the majority of cases, these changes are permanent.

✏ EXAM TASK: Speaking (Part 2)

6   **Prepare answers to the questions. In pairs, take turns to talk about the topic for one to two minutes.**

Describe a bad habit that you have changed.

You should say:
   what the habit was
   why you believed that you should change it
   what approaches you decided to use
and explain why you think these worked.

7   **Discuss in small groups.**

a) Why do you think people start bad habits?

b) Why do they not always manage to give bad habits up?

c) What tips would you have for someone who is trying to break a bad habit?

The container revolution

1 **Complete the definitions with the words in the box.**

> cargo   freight   a shipping container   a transport network

a) .... is a term for all goods that are transported by air, sea, or land, and the system of moving them.

b) .... is a word used for goods that are transported by air or sea.

c) .... is a standard-sized metal box used for transporting goods.

d) .... is a system of routes which cross or are connected to each other.

2 **Read the text about different modes of transport for freight. Discuss in pairs. Which modes of freight transportation are compared? Which benefits and drawbacks are mentioned?**

> 90% of world trade is transported by sea. Maersk's latest container ships have a capacity equivalent to 18,000 twenty-foot containers. Maersk, a Danish company, has also recently lowered its sailing speed slightly in order to cut fuel consumption and lower CO_2 emissions.
>
> The key argument for sending goods by plane has always been the speed of delivery. Many consider that with air freight, there is also less damage to goods. However, the cost of air freight is higher since the cargo space of an aeroplane is significantly smaller than that of a cargo ship.
>
> Rail travel is particularly useful for trade between countries with common borders. The CO_2 emissions for trains are far lower than those for road transport. Experts predict that rail projects such as the Trans-Asian Railway (TAR), which aims to create a rail freight network across Europe and Asia, mean that rail transport has a strong future on both a regional and global level.

3 **Check your grammar!** **Answer the questions about the underlined noun phrases in the text.**

a) Write definitions for the underlined words.

b) What parts of speech are the underlined words?

c) What would the plural form of each underlined item be?

> **Grammar tip**
>
> Nouns and noun phrases are commonly found in academic writing. They are used to make a text sound less personal or to express a lot of information concisely.

✎ **EXAM TASK:**
Reading (Matching sentence endings)

4 **Read the text about the development of container shipping on page 41. Complete each sentence with the correct ending, A – G. There are more endings than you need.**

	A world trade.
1 The containerisation of shipping has accelerated	**B** a container shipping revolution.
2 As far as transport is concerned, people have always recognised	**C** the importance of oceans.
3 In the twentieth century the transport industry underwent	**D** the tourist economy.
4 These days ships do not frequently offer	**E** the unloading of cargo.
5 Cruise ships make a significant contribution to	**F** transport costs.
	G long-distance ferry routes.

Throughout history the oceans have been important to <u>people around the world</u> as a means of transportation. Unlike a few decades ago, however, ships are now carrying more goods than people. As a result of the <u>increasing demand</u> for intercontinental air travel, sea travel has become limited to shorter trips, such as ferry services across the Mediterranean and recreational cruises. The latter have experienced <u>a tremendous</u> <u>boom</u> and represent an increasingly lucrative source of tourist income.

Container shipping was first introduced in the USA during the 1960s. A <u>transport entrepreneur</u>, Malcolm McLean, bought a steamship company with the intention of transporting entire <u>truck trailers with cargo inside</u>. He realised it would be much simpler and quicker to have one container that could be lifted from a vehicle directly on to a ship without first having to unload its contents. <u>McLean's idea that containers could be moved seamlessly between ships, trucks and trains</u> has revolutionised global cargo shipping, bringing about vast <u>improvements in</u> efficiency. Many experts consider containerisation to be one of the key developments in transport of the twentieth century. As a result of <u>increasingly globalised markets</u>, shipping volumes have soared. World trade since the 1950s has more than trebled to 45 per cent of the global GDP.

Reproduced by kind permission of World Ocean Review 1, maribus gGmbH, Hamburg 2010

5a **Read the Grammar reference. Choose examples for each point from the underlined phrases in the text in exercise 4. Add them to the Grammar reference.**

Grammar reference: nouns and noun phrases

Noun phrases

- Nouns are often preceded by adjectives or adjective phrases, e.g. **(1)** .... , including adverb-adjective combinations, e.g. **(2)** ....
- Nouns can be preceded by a verb or verb +-*ing* form, e.g. **(3)** ....
- Nouns can also be preceded by other nouns, e.g. **(4)** .... Some of these combinations are frequently used together and act like a single word, known as a compound noun. Compound nouns are sometimes written as two words, one word or hyphenated, e.g. *car park, bathroom, check-out*. Look up the spelling in a good dictionary.
- The first noun in a noun + noun combination is usually singular, e.g. *container shipping (~~containers shipping~~)*.
- Sometimes we can use noun + possessive *'s* instead of noun + noun to give the idea of belonging, physical characteristics or relationships. We often use this when the first noun refers to a person, group, organisation, animal or country and to refer to time, e.g. *McLean's idea, Maersk's latest container ships, a cat's tail, in five years' time*.
- To give a possessive meaning with other nouns or a long noun phrase, we often prefer noun + *of* + noun, e.g. *the employees of the trucking entrepreneur (~~the trucking entrepreneur's employees~~), the cargo space of an aeroplane (~~an aeroplane's cargo space~~)*. This also has the effect of making a text sound more formal.
- Prepositional phrases (phrases headed by a preposition), e.g. *across the Mediterranean,* commonly follow other nouns. Prepositional phrases following nouns can often be used instead of a defining relative clause, e.g. **(5)** .... (= people who live around the world), **(6)** .... (= truck trailers which have their cargo inside).
- Some nouns are always followed by the same preposition(s), e.g. *means of, cost(s) of, argument for, damage to,* **(7)** .... Learn nouns together with the prepositions which follow them.
- We can combine several of these features in a noun phrase, e.g. *an increasingly lucrative source of tourist income.*

Noun clauses

Some nouns are followed by noun clauses which give more information about the noun. These noun clauses act like a very long subject. Some nouns which are often used in this way are:

- *(the) argument / belief / claim / fact / idea / possibility / risk / statement / warning* + *that*-clause, e.g. **(8)** .... *has revolutionised global cargo shipping.*
- *(the) description / discussion / example / idea / issue / problem / question / understanding* + *of* + question word-clause, e.g. ***The issue of how to accelerate the unloading of cargo*** *was solved by McLean.*

5b **Look at options A – G in the exam task in exercise 4 again. How many of these are noun phrases?**

6 **Correct twelve errors in the use of noun phrases and clauses in this text.**

Oceans shipping can roughly be divided into two sectors – liquid cargo, such as crude oil, and dry cargo. Dry cargo is made up of bulk cargo which is transported unpackaged in large quantities, the five most important being iron's ore, coal, grain, phosphates and bauxite. Other dry cargo includes a variety of goods packed chiefly in containers.

Container shipping's drawback is that adequate port facilities have special cranes, storage space and railway systems are required. For this reason container traffic initially became established on only the busiest shipping routes. There are in fact a relative small number of principal transport routes. The busiest are the approaches to Europe and East Asia's ports, particularly Japan, but also Shanghai, Singapore and Hong Kong and the United States.

World shipping is responsible for about 3 per cent of global CO_2 emissions. Experts predict that in the time of thirty years, unless further measures are taken to protect the climate, emissions from shipping could approximately treble. Recent innovate in design, such as Maersk's 400-metre Triple-E class container ships, are aimed chiefly at dramatically reducing fuel's consumption.

For shipping companies, the issue that what to do with returning vessels is of constant concern. This affects the bulk cargo sector in particular. Minerals resources are often geographically distant from where they are processed, meaning many large ships transport cargo in only one direction and the shipping company is left to cover the costs to returning the empty ships.

Grammar tip

A noun + noun phrase can be used for expressions of measurement. Note the use of hyphens and the singular first noun, e.g. *a 400-metre ship, a thirteen-year-old boy.*

✏ EXAM TASK: Writing (Task 1)

7   **The graph below shows the growth in international sea freight over a period of 34 years. Summarise the information by selecting and reporting the main features and make comparisons where relevant. Include noun phrases and noun clauses in your answer.**

International sea freight 1980 to 2014 (millions of tons loaded)

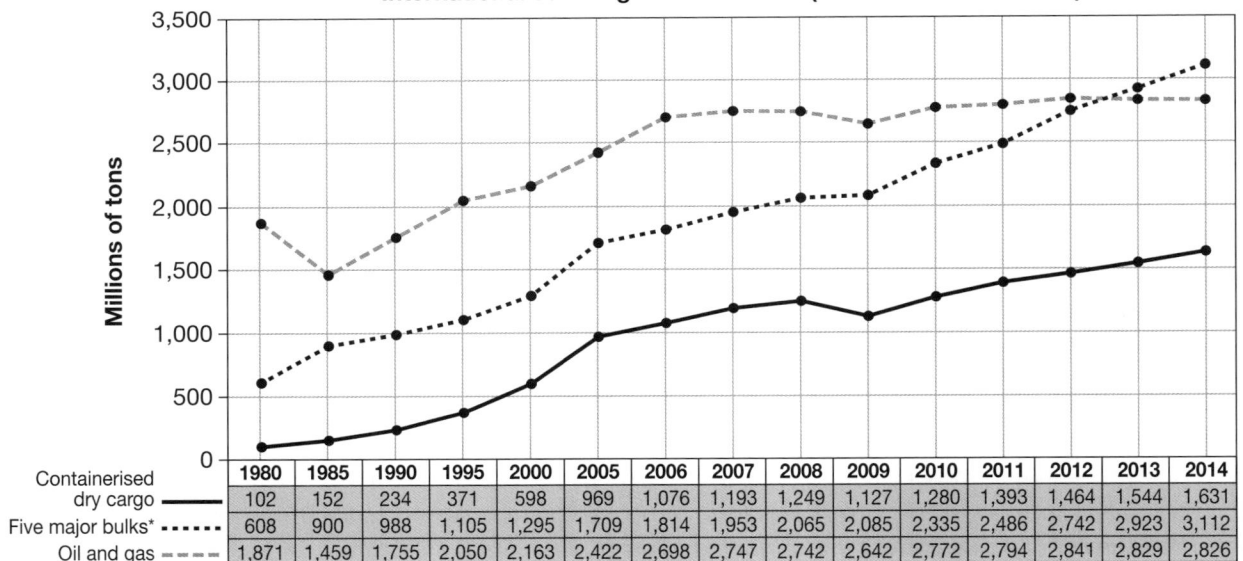

	1980	1985	1990	1995	2000	2005	2006	2007	2008	2009	2010	2011	2012	2013	2014
Containerised dry cargo ——	102	152	234	371	598	969	1,076	1,193	1,249	1,127	1,280	1,393	1,464	1,544	1,631
Five major bulks* ······	608	900	988	1,105	1,295	1,709	1,814	1,953	2,065	2,085	2,335	2,486	2,742	2,923	3,112
Oil and gas ----	1,871	1,459	1,755	2,050	2,163	2,422	2,698	2,747	2,742	2,642	2,772	2,794	2,841	2,829	2,826

*Five major types of bulk cargo: iron ore, coal, grain, phosphates and bauxite.

Biodiversity and food

1a **Complete the definitions with the words in the box.**

> a community   an ecosystem   a habitat   an organism   a species

a) .... is a plant, an animal, a human or any other living thing, including bacteria.

b) .... is a group of animals or plants whose members are similar and can breed together.

c) .... is a place where an organism lives.

d) .... describes all the different organisms that live together in a habitat.

e) .... is a term for the habitats and communities that exist and interact in a certain area.

1b **Discuss in pairs. What do you understand by the term 'biodiversity'? Why is biodiversity on Earth important?**

Biodiversity ...

... is the variety of different species living in an ecosystem. The greater the number of different species in an ecosystem, the greater its biodiversity. The term is also used to describe the variety of ecosystems and habitats on Earth as a whole.

Humans <u>depend on</u> an array of food and materials to lead healthy and happy lives. Most medical discoveries to cure or <u>guard against</u> diseases are the result of research into plant and animal biology. Different species and ecosystems have different roles, which together make life on Earth possible, for example wetland plants <u>soak</u> water <u>up</u> and filter out harmful pollutants, while rainforests <u>provide us with</u> oxygen to breathe.

The incredible success of the human species actually risks contributing to its downfall. The biodiversity we see today is a result of 3.5 billion years of evolution. Extinction is a natural pattern of life on Earth. Species <u>die out</u> because of natural shifts in the environment that <u>come about</u> over long periods of time. However, due to humanity's over-exploitation of natural resources and unsustainable development, species are becoming extinct and natural ecosystems are degrading at an unprecedented rate. It is estimated that the extinction rate of current species is between 1,000 and 10,000 times higher than it would naturally be. All of this <u>adds up to</u> a situation which could have severe consequences for the environment and human health and livelihoods. It is now time for the human race to <u>take on</u> the challenge of preserving biodiversity on Earth.

2 **Check your grammar!** **Match the definitions and synonyms with the underlined verbs in the text. What type of verbs are underlined in the text?**

a) become extinct

b) produce (a particular result)

c) need the support of (in order to exist)

d) supply (someone) with

e) prevent (from happening)

f) happen (usually unplanned)

g) agree to = (take responsibility for)

h) absorb (a liquid)

Grammar tip

The meaning of some multi-word verbs is straightforward, e.g. *go in* (= enter). However, others are difficult to work out just by looking at the separate meanings of the verb or the particle, e.g. *set off* (= leave). Learn each multi-word verb as a separate item of vocabulary.

3 Read the Grammar reference. Look at the lists of verbs below. Add a heading for each list of verbs, using the Grammar reference to help you.

Grammar reference: multi-word verbs

Multi-word verbs are two- or three-word verbs comprising of a verb (e.g. *look*) + particle(s) (= preposition / adverb, e.g. *after, up*). Some uses of multi-word verbs are informal, e.g. *Check this out!* Some have a one-word synonym which is often more formal in style, e.g. *We mustn't **put** this **off** any longer.* (informal) / *It is essential not to **postpone** the decision further.* (more formal) However, this is not true of all multi-word verbs, and they are used regularly in academic writing.

- Some multi-word verbs can have more than one meaning, e.g. *They've taken on a new challenge.* (*take on* = accept / agree to) *They've taken on two new members of staff.* (*take on* = employ) Some verbs can take different particles to form verbs with different meanings, e.g. *work on, work for, work out*.
- Just like single-word verbs, some multi-word verbs are used in particular verb patterns, e.g. *I keep on learning.* (*keep on* + verb + *-ing* form) *Sethi points out that Arabica is now threatened by extinction.* (*point out* + *that*-clause) *We could not work out what had happened.* (*work out* + question-word clause)

Prepositional verbs

Prepositional verbs are formed with a verb + preposition, e.g. *rely on, guard against*. Prepositional verbs are followed by a noun or pronoun, which usually comes immediately after the preposition, e.g. *Humans depend on **an array of food and materials**. / Humans depend on **them***.

- Some prepositional verbs take two objects, e.g. *Rainforests provide **us** with **oxygen***.

Phrasal verbs

Phrasal verbs are formed with a verb + adverb, e.g. *come about, die out, take on*.

- Phrasal verbs can be intransitive (= they don't take an object), e.g. *Species **die out** because of natural shifts in the environment*. They can also be transitive (= they take an object), e.g. *She's **taken on the challenge**.* Some phrasal verbs have both transitive and intransitive uses, e.g. *Wake up!* or *Can someone wake **me** up, please?*
- Unlike prepositional verbs, the object of a phrasal verb can go in two different positions, e.g. *They soak up **water**.* (object after the adverb 'up') or *They soak **water** up.* (object before the adverb 'up'). When the object is a longer phrase, we prefer to have it after the adverb, e.g. *It is time for the human race to take on **the challenge of maintaining biodiversity on Earth**.* If the object is a personal pronoun, it comes before the adverb, e.g. *She's taken **it** on.*

Three-word verbs

Some verbs have two particles, making them three-word verbs, e.g *add up to*. The object follows the second particle, e.g. *All of this adds up to **a situation which could have severe consequences for the environment***.

1
....
add up to X
come up with X
....

2
....
come about
die out
....

3
....
soak up X, soak X up
take on X, take X on
work out X, work X out
turn X into, turn into X
try X out, try out X
cut X down, cut down X

4
....
depend on X
guard against X
look after X
lead to X
....

5
....
provide X with Y
protect X from Y
deprive X of Y
....

4a **Work in pairs. Read the article and think of a title for it.**

It may not seem, from the overwhelming choice of products that are available in many grocery stores, that there is a lack of diversity in food. Yet the Food and Agriculture Organisation of the United Nations reports that 95 per cent of the calories consumed worldwide <u>come from</u> a mere thirty species. One breed of cow, the Holstein-Friesian, <u>supplies us with</u> 90 per cent of dairy products. Recent research shows that the global trend in food is towards five major crops: wheat, rice, corn, soya beans and palm oil.

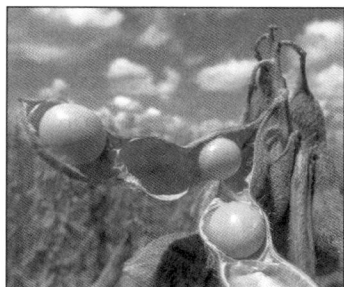

soya bean plant

At the University of Melbourne in Australia, journalist and educator Simran Sethi has conducted research on the loss of global agricultural biodiversity. She was shocked by the seriousness of what she was discovering and knew it was time to <u>speak out</u>. The drawback of monocropping is that climate change, a single pest or a rampaging plant disease could threaten our global food supply. Agricultural biodiversity increases the resilience of our food supply by ensuring we have foods that could exist under future conditions. Equally if we <u>leave</u> certain species <u>out</u> of production, we will not have access to traits that can be used to make existing crops more drought-tolerant or pest-resistant.

In her reports, Sethi <u>points out</u> that some of our best-loved foods are at risk. Arabica, one of the world's most popular coffee beans, is now threatened by extinction due to climate change and deforestation in Ethiopia. In addition, cacao trees, from which chocolate is derived, are pollinated by an unremarkable fly called the chocolate midge. However, as cacao growers attempt to <u>keep up with</u> consumer demand, they are destroying midge habitats.

Sethi argues that <u>facing up to</u> the risks of this situation is crucial. The reduction in diversity of what we grow and eat, combined with industrialisation, is efficient from a business perspective, but <u>relying on</u> fewer kinds of foods to feed ourselves is not a good model for survival.

4b **Look at the multi-word verbs underlined in the text. Check the meaning of any that you do not know. Write each of the multi-word verbs in the appropriate box in exercise 3. Look in a good dictionary to check whether each multi-word verb takes an object (X) and the position of any object.**

5 **Correct the uses of the multi-word verbs in these sentences.**

a) The world population is expected to rise to 9.6 billion people by 2050. Working out that to feed the growing population, while also looking valuable ecosystems after, is one of the greatest challenges of our era.

b) Intensive farming practices produce more and cheaper food which has helped feed a booming human population but has led out a huge number of environmental problems. One of these problems is the loss of forests. We are cutting down them to provide grazing land for animals.

c) The loss of local ingredients means that some local cultures and cuisines are also in danger of die out, depriving future generations with valuable knowledge.

d) Around the world people are coming up initiatives to support traditional farming practices and establishing protected areas – areas which are protected of human activity – in order to maintain biodiversity.

e) For some, the choice of food products has turned it into a symbol for saving our planet. They recommend trying out of new ingredients and buying ingredients from small producers.

✎ EXAM TASK: Speaking (Part 3)

6 **Work in pairs. Discuss the questions.**

Why do some people prefer cooking to eating out?

Do people throw away too much food?

Should supermarkets increase or cut back on the choice of food available?

Megacities

1 **Check your grammar!** Look at the line graph and complete the sentences in the description. Use one word only in each gap. What type of word is needed in each gap?

Urban population by income group, 1950–2050

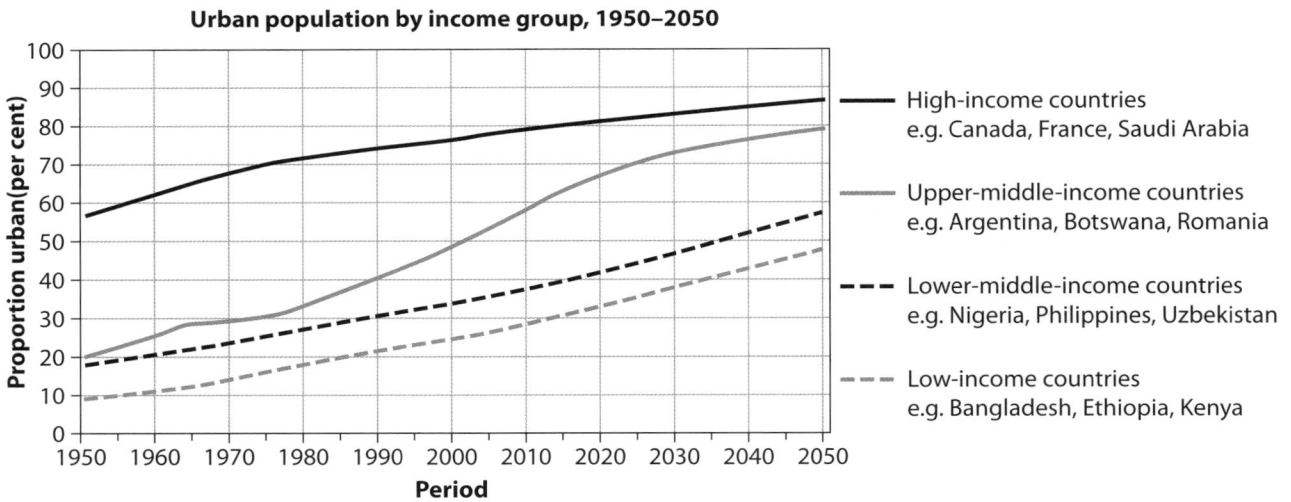

- High-income countries
  e.g. Canada, France, Saudi Arabia
- Upper-middle-income countries
  e.g. Argentina, Botswana, Romania
- Lower-middle-income countries
  e.g. Nigeria, Philippines, Uzbekistan
- Low-income countries
  e.g. Bangladesh, Ethiopia, Kenya

This graph shows the proportion of the world's population living in cities. It illustrates the growth

(1) .... urbanisation **(2)** .... 1950 and projected rates of urbanisation up

(3) .... 2050. In 2014, **(4)** .... high-income countries and upper-middle-income countries,

the majority **(5)** .... the population lived in urban areas: 80% and just **(6)** 60%,

respectively. The urban transition in higher income countries started many decades ago: 57% of the

population in these countries lived in urban areas **(7)** .... 1950 and the level **(8)** ....

urbanisation is expected to reach 86% by 2050. Upper-middle-income countries have experienced the fastest

pace of urbanisation since 1970, but the pace will slow **(9)** .... the coming decades.

(10) .... contrast, lower-middle and low-income countries are projected to experience the fastest

urbanisation rates. In 1950, lower-middle-income countries started with a comparable level of urbanisation

to upper-middle-income countries of **(11)** .... 20%. However, the urbanisation process has

been slower in lower-middle-income countries where 39% of the population was living in urban areas in

2014, an increase **(12)** .... 19%. Low-income countries started with a low level **(13)** ....

urbanisation in 1950 – **(14)** .... just below 10%. However, the period **(15)** .... 1990 and

2014 saw a dramatic increase **(16)** .... the numbers of people living in cities from around 20%

(17) .... 30%. 50% **(18)** .... the population in low-income countries is projected to live

in urban areas by 2050.

Grammar tip

below and *under* can both mean 'lower than'; *above* and *over* can both mean 'higher than'. For measurements, we often prefer 'below' and 'above', e.g. *below zero, above average*; for age and speed, 'under' and 'over' are generally used, e.g. *under 18* (= less than 18), *over 70 mph* (= more than 70).

2 Look at the chart. Discuss in pairs. How many megacities were there in 1970 and in 2014? How many of the 1970 and 2014 megacities do you think you can name?

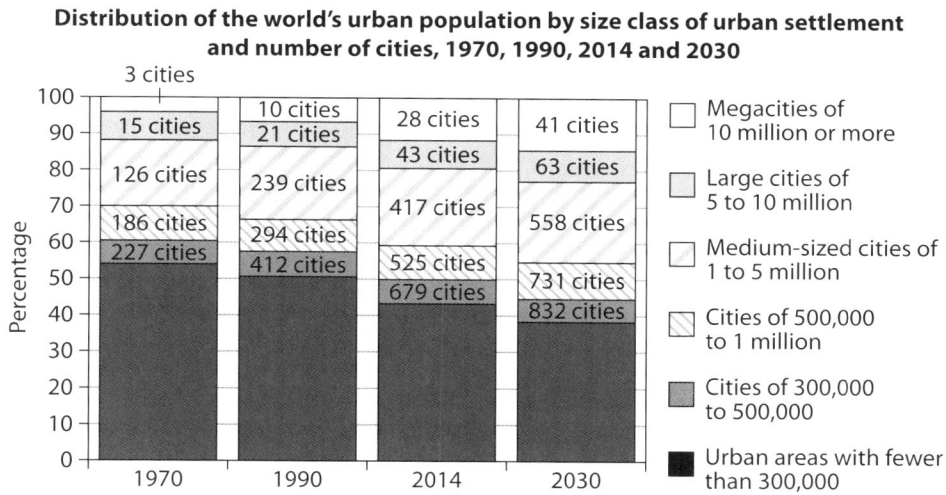

Distribution of the world's urban population by size class of urban settlement and number of cities, 1970, 1990, 2014 and 2030

3 cities

	1970	1990	2014	2030
Megacities of 10 million or more	15 cities	10 cities / 21 cities	28 cities	41 cities
Large cities of 5 to 10 million	126 cities	239 cities	43 cities	63 cities
Medium-sized cities of 1 to 5 million	186 cities	294 cities	417 cities	558 cities
Cities of 500,000 to 1 million	227 cities	412 cities	525 cities	731 cities
Cities of 300,000 to 500,000			679 cities	832 cities
Urban areas with fewer than 300,000				

(Percentage axis 0–100)

3 Choose a phrase from one of the boxes to complete each sentence.

> **A** different from   crucial for   responsible for

> **B** availability of   effects on   proximity to   improvements in

> **C** on average   in contrast   one in eight   at very different rates

---

THE NUMBER AND GROWTH OF LARGE CITIES

Today's 28 megacities are quite **(1)** .... each other in terms of both size and growth paths. They rank from 10.2 million to 37.8 million inhabitants and together they are home to around **(2)** .... of the world's urban dwellers. Over the past four decades, they have grown **(3)** .... For example, between 1970 and 1990, the Japanese megacity of Osaka expanded slowly, at a rate below 1% per year **(4)** .... **(5)** .... African and Asian megacities, such as Lagos and Dhaka, had annual growth rates of above 6%. A multitude of factors can influence the rate at which cities grow, such as geographic location, climate, natural resources, such as the **(6)** .... of water or the lack of it, the types of industries that characterise the city's economy and the **(7)** .... other cities in the region. When megacities have 20 million or more inhabitants, they are also referred to as 'meta' or 'hyper' cities.

POPULATION CHANGE AFFECTS EDUCATION PLANNING

The continued growth of urban areas has implications for education system planning. Globally, much of urban growth is due to natural population growth and migration from rural areas is also **(8)** .... some of the increase. Population growth has significant **(9)** .... education and requires careful governance at a local and national level. Education and lifelong learning are **(10)** .... helping government address urban challenges and can have positive effects, such as reducing crime, tackling inequality and reminding communities of the many opportunities of urbanisation. **(11)** .... education planning will result in cities which are more inclusive, prosperous and safer places to live.

Grammar tip

Some nouns may take a preposition, but the verb from the same word family does not, e.g. *There is a lack of water* (*lack* (n) + *of*). *The city lacks water.* (*lack* (v), no preposition).

---

4 Read the Grammar reference. Look back at the word boxes in exercise 3. Which point in the Grammar reference does each box give examples of?

Grammar reference: prepositions

- Many prepositions are single words, e.g. *about, across, as, at, before, below, between, by, during, for, in, into, near, of, on, outside, over, past, through, towards, up, with, within, without*. However sometimes groups of two or three words can act like one-word prepositions, e.g. *due to, such as, in terms of, as well as*.

- Some nouns and adjectives are followed by particular prepositions, e.g. *type of, implications for, a role in; aware of, good at, keen on*.

- Some verbs take a particular preposition, e.g. *refer to, result in*. Prepositional verbs are followed by a noun phrase or pronoun, which usually comes immediately after the preposition, e.g. *This will result in **more inclusive and prosperous cities***. Some prepositional verbs take two objects, e.g. *reminding **communities** of **the many opportunities***.

- There is sometimes a choice of preposition after a noun, verb or adjective. The different options may have the same meaning, e.g. *This chart illustrates the growth in / of urbanisation* or the uses may be different, e.g. *He cares for her.* (care for = look after) *He cares about her.* (care about = feel that someone or something is important)

- *Wh*-questions can end on the preposition when the question word is the object of the preposition, e.g. ***Which city do you come from?*** This also happens in indirect *wh*-questions, e.g. *Can you tell me **which** city you come **from**?*

- When a relative pronoun is the object of a preposition, the preposition often goes at the end of the clause, e.g. *A lot of factors can influence the rate **which** cities grow **at***. In more formal language, the preposition often precedes the relative pronoun (*which* or *whom*), e.g. *A multitude of factors can influence the **rate at which** cities grow*.

Prepositional phrases

- Prepositions are often followed by a noun phrase to form a prepositional phrase, e.g. *in contrast, for example, under age, out of date, by accident*.

- Prepositions can also be followed by a pronoun, a phrase or clause, e.g. *water or the lack of **it**, urban areas **with ten million inhabitants or more***.

- When prepositions are followed by a verb, the verb usually takes the *-ing* form, e.g. *a crucial role **in tackling** inequality* (*a crucial role to tackle*). In negative forms, *not* comes between the preposition and the *-ing* form, e.g. *a policy of **not** accepting discrimination*.

Grammar tip

Learn prepositions in context. Check their use in a good dictionary. Read widely to find prepositions used naturally.

✏ EXAM TASK: Speaking (Part 2)

5 Prepare answers to the questions. In pairs, take turns to talk about the topic for one to two minutes.

> Describe a city you have enjoyed going to recently.
>
> You should say:
>   where the city is
>   when you visited
>   which places you were particularly interested in
> and explain why you liked this city.

6 There is one preposition missing in each of the sentences in this text about the transformation of the city of Medellin. In pairs, read the text and add the prepositions.

The UNESCO Global Network of Learning Cities (GNLC) encourages cities to put education and lifelong learning the heart of their development and become 'learning cities'.

An initiative in Medellín, Colombia, has integrated education into urban planning dramatic results. In the 1980s, Medellín was the headquarters of Pablo Escobar's drug cartel and infamous its narcoterrorism and corruption. After Escobar's death in 1993, the city established a progressive agenda, involving communities in the expansion public spaces and services. The programme included a metro system, innovative buildings and parks which doubled learning spaces, and the construction of 120 new public schools.

It is Mayor Sergio Fajardo whom much of the success of the initiative has been attributed. His visionary leadership, Medellin has been transformed into one of the most innovative cities in the world. As a result there has been a dramatic decrease the incidence of crime and violence. To reduce inequality, Fajardo focused improving public education, rather than supporting private education. Over the past two decades, the government allocated to 40% of its municipal budget to education. The investment programme targeted the poorest areas providing a message of public support in a place once belonging crime gangs.

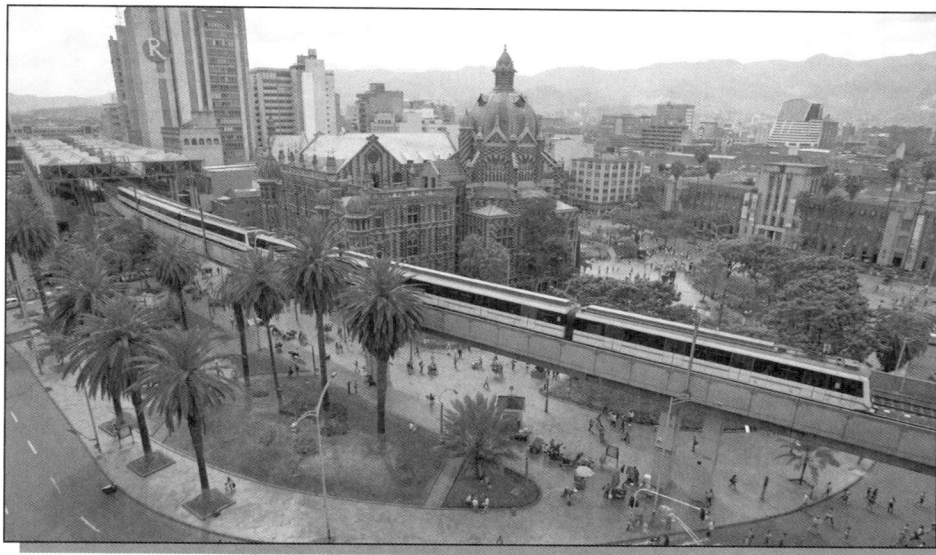

Grammar tip

We can follow some nouns with infinitive + preposition. The preposition is sometimes left out, particularly after the noun *place*, e.g. *Everyone needs a safe place to live (in).*

✏ EXAM TASK: Speaking (Part 3)

7 Work in pairs. Discuss the questions.

What is important to you when choosing a place to live?

What are the advantages or disadvantages of living in a city?

Do you think some cities are in danger of becoming too large? Why? / Why not?

Sensational news

1   Work in pairs. Read the newspaper report and discuss your reaction to it.

How much does a muffin cost?

Answer: More than $16 if you are <u>at a US government conference</u>. Muffins <u>probably</u> cost just over $2 at your average coffee shop, but unbelievably the Justice Department paid seven to eight times as much at a conference held at the Capital Hilton <u>in Washington</u>. A report just released by the Justice Department auditors points to 'wasteful or extravagant spending' at a number of different conferences <u>over the last decade</u>.

2   Read the text below. According to the writer, what is the most significant thing about the news story?

The media could not believe it. Muffins that were <u>apparently</u> costing a government department $16 each. The highly extravagant price tag for a simple baked good was undoubtedly the perfect symbol of bureaucratic largesse. Unfortunately, it wasn't true. <u>Three days later</u>, Hilton Hotels (which hosted the conference) clarified that the $16 charge was for a full continental breakfast plus tax. Instead of a detailed invoice, the hotel just listed the charge as 'muffins'. However, the damage had been done. Almost <u>immediately</u>, some commentators had called for resignations, while others had even used the story to call for a stop to tax rises.

It also shows how the political and media communities are <u>usually</u> quick to trumpet an outrage-inducing story, but don't often bother to set the record straight. According to one journalist, there were 223 stories that mentioned the $16 muffins <u>between September 20th and September 28th</u>. Of those stories, around three quarters reported the issue <u>unfavourably</u> or didn't even mention the Hilton hotel's response. Only a minority of stories offered an explanation for the cost of the muffins or subsequently attempted to correct the record.

3a   **Check your grammar!** Read the information about adverbs and complete the table with the examples of the adverbs underlined in the two texts above. Check your answers in the key.

Adverbs are used for a wide range of functions when describing an action, event or process.
They can be a single word or a phrase: many prepositional phrases of time and place function as adverbs.

Adverbs commonly indicate:	Examples:
manner	
place	
time (including duration)	
frequency	
degree of certainty (possibility and probability)	
viewpoint	

3b Complete the sentences about the position of adverbs, using the adverbs underlined in the texts in exercises 1 and 2 to help you.

There are three main positions for adverbs: at the start of a clause, at the end of a clause or in mid-position. Many adverbs can be used in any of the three positions depending on the context or on the writer's style.

- In mid-position, adverbs are generally used before one-part verbs, e.g. *The hotel **just listed** the charge as 'muffins'*. However, the adverb comes after the verb *be*, auxiliary verbs and modal verbs, e.g. *Some stories **didn't even** mention the Hilton hotel's response*. When there is more than one auxiliary verb, the adverb usually comes after the first auxiliary, e.g. *A report which **has just been** released …*
- Adverbs of time and place usually come at the end of a clause, but are sometimes used **(1)** ....
- Adverbs of frequency and adverbs which refer to a degree of certainty often go **(2)** ....
- Adverbs of viewpoint are used **(3)** .... , but they can also be used at the start of a sentence since they may refer to the whole idea.

4 Match the definitions with the examples.

Adverbs and adverb phrases (shown in bold) can be used to modify a number of different parts of speech or parts of a sentence, such as:

1 a verb	**a) Unfortunately**, it wasn't true.
2 an adjective	**b) almost** immediately
3 another adverb	**c)** Muffins **probably** cost just over $2 at your average coffee shop …
4 a prepositional phrase	**d)** …but **unbelievably** the Justice Department paid $16 each.
5 a noun phrase	**e) only** a minority of stories
6 a clause	**f) just** over two dollars
7 the whole sentence	**g) extremely** wasteful

5 Work in pairs. Read the Grammar reference and look at the lists of adverbs below. Number the groups of adverbs 1 – 5 (5 = strongest degree).

Grammar reference: adverbs of degree

Adverbs of degree describe to what degree something happens and are commonly used before an adjective, e.g. *highly extravagant*. They can intensify or reduce the strength of the word they precede.

- Stronger adverbs of degree, e.g. *absolutely*, are not used with all adjectives. For example, we say *absolutely amazing*, but *highly dangerous*. Learn adverb + adjective collocations as you come across them.
- *quite* has two meanings depending on whether it is used with a gradable or non-gradable adjective: *quite good* = 'almost very good' (*good* is a gradable adjective – it has a wide range of meaning); *quite impossible* = 'completely impossible' (*impossible* is an absolute or non-gradable adjective).

a) very, really ....

b) hardly, scarcely ....

c) absolutely, completely, entirely, extremely, greatly, highly, quite, totally ....

d) almost, fairly, nearly, practically, relatively, slightly ....

e) partly, quite, rather ....

6 Read the Grammar reference and complete the information with the words in the box.

> a short time ago   object   in mid-position   place the focus   similar   surprising

Grammar reference: focussing adverbs

Focussing adverbs **(1)** .... on a particular part of the clause. Common focussing adverbs include: *also, either … or, neither … nor, especially, particularly, even, just, only, largely, mainly, mostly.*

- *also, too* and *as well* have **(2)** .... meanings; *also* can be used at the beginning of a clause or in mid-position, e.g. *It also shows how … . Also, it shows how … ; as well* and *too* usually go at the end of a clause.

- Use *even* to express a **(3)** .... extreme, e.g. … *while others had even used the story to call for …* (= more than is expected); … *they didn't even mention the Hilton hotel's response.* (= less than is expected). It is most commonly used with a verb in mid-position or in front of a noun.

- *just* has a number of different uses, e.g. *The hotel just listed the charge as 'muffins'.* (*just* = 'only' or 'nothing more than') *The report has just been released.* (*just* = **(4)** '.................................')

- *only* is often used with the subject that it refers to, e.g. *Only a minority of stories … .* When *only* is used to focus on a part of the sentence, it is typically used **(5)** .... , e.g.*The hotel only listed the charge as 'muffins'.*

- We do not usually put adverbs between a verb and its **(6)** .... , e.g. *I often read newspapers.* (*I read often newspapers*) or between a verb and an *-ing* form. In academic writing, we prefer not to put an adverb between a verb and a *that*-clause / *to*-infinitive or to split an infinitive verb form with an adverb, e.g. *They subsequently attempted to correct the record. / They attempted to correct the record subsequently.* (*They attempted to subsequently correct … / They attempted subsequently to correct …*)

7 Read the text and add each of the adverbs in brackets to the preceding underlined phrase. It may be possible to put the adverbs in more than one position with a change in emphasis.

A very human quality?

(1) <u>Sensationalism is nothing new.</u> (*definitely*) Journalism professor, Mitchell Stephens, from the New York University writes in his book *A History of News* that sensationalism has been around ever since early humans began telling stories.

(2) <u>Criticism of sensationalism has a long history.</u> (*also*) **(3)** <u>The Roman philosopher Cicero complained</u> (*even*) that the *Acta Diurna* – handwritten sheets that were the equivalent of ancient Rome's daily paper –
(4) <u>reported the latest gossip about gladiators</u> (*only*) **(5)** <u>and neglected to report real news</u> (*frequently*).

Stephens believes that sensationalism is unavoidable since humans are hard-wired, **(6)** <u>for reasons of natural selection</u> (*probably*), to be alert to sensations, **(7)** <u>those involving relationships and danger</u> (*particularly*).
(8) <u>Sensationalism promotes the spread of information</u> (*arguably*) to less literate audiences.
(9) <u>While some of the stories are believable,</u> (*scarcely*) **(10)** <u>others help us to establish</u> (*actually*) or question society's norms and boundaries.

Sensational stories are the junk food of our news diet, **(11)** <u>the sugary dessert that you devour.</u> (*eagerly*) You know **(12)** <u>it's bad for you,</u> (*quite*) but **(13)** <u>you can have a salad tomorrow.</u> (*always*) Despite what high-minded critics might say, an interest in the sensational
(14) <u>is a quality that is very human</u> (*just*).

Grammar tip

There are many adverbs which can be used to reveal a speaker's / writer's attitude towards an event, action or process, e.g. *actually, in fact, indeed; clearly, obviously, of course, undoubtedly, not surprisingly; (un)fortunately, luckily, preferably; apparently, arguably, supposedly; personally; literally.*

8 Complete the text with the adverbs in the box.

accurately   clearly   consistently   extremely   largely   only   relatively   significantly   steadily

Percentage of respondents with a great deal / fair amount of trust in the media

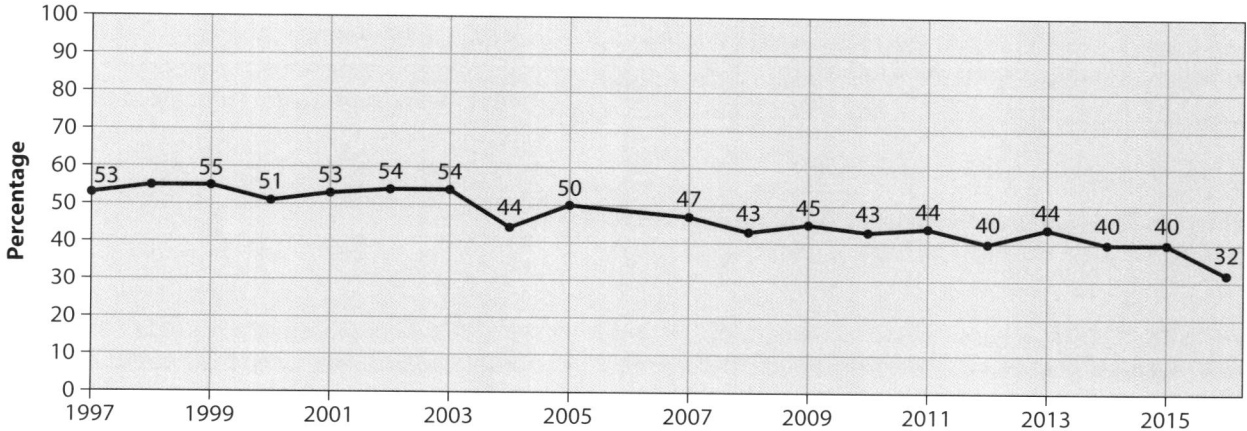

The American public's trust in the media has fallen to its lowest point for over 40 years, according to a 2016 Gallup public opinion poll, with **(1)** .... 32% saying they have a great deal or fair amount of trust in the media. In 1972, the Gallup Poll began asking the American public how much confidence they had in the mass media to report the news **(2)** .... and fairly. After staying **(3)** .... stable through the late 1990s and into the early years of the new century, Americans' trust in the media has since fallen slowly and **(4)** .... Since 2007, it has **(5)** .... been below a majority level. Accuracy is **(6)** .... the most important component of trust in news reporting, according to a separate study carried out by the Media Insight Project. Nearly 90% of Americans say it is **(7)** .... or very important that the media get their facts correct. About four in ten say they can remember a specific incident that **(8)** .... lowered their confidence in the media. These incidents were **(9)** .... ones that dealt with accuracy or were perceived to be one-sided.

✎ EXAM TASK: Writing (Task 2)

9   Write about the topic below. Give reasons for your answer and include any relevant examples from your own knowledge or experience. Include some of the types of adverb which have been practised in this lesson. Underline the examples you use.

> The media devotes too much time to reporting sensational stories. Yet issues that have a significant effect on our lives and the lives of people worldwide receive comparatively little attention.
>
> To what extent do you agree or disagree?

The skills of the locksmith

1 **Look at the words below. Which of these are paid professions? What do the other words mean?**

> locksmith   silversmith   songsmith   wordsmith

2a **Check your grammar!** **Read the text and answer the questions.**

a) Which skills are essential for a locksmith?

b) What advice is given?

c) What is a locksmith not allowed to do?

d) Which verbs are used in the text to indicate …

… strong obligation?

… necessity?

… advice?

> *Smith* is the most prevalent surname in the United Kingdom, Australia and the United States. It is derived from the Old English word meaning 'someone who works in metal'.

TopJob.com

What is a locksmith?

People often call a locksmith when they lock themselves out of their car, home or office. Locksmiths have the difficult job of unlocking doors, safes and locks that are jammed or broken.

TOP JOB ☰
Careers advice

Skills & knowledge

A locksmith must have good carpentry and metalwork skills. Locksmiths need to have good motor skills to disassemble padlocks, safe locks and door locks and gain access to tight areas using specialised tools. A locksmith has to use computers to reset electronic codes for high-tech locking systems.

Qualifications & training

There are a number of specialised qualifications accredited by the MLA (Master Locksmiths Association). You must not set up in business as a locksmith without first gaining these. If you are considering a career as a locksmith, you should contact the MLA for further information.

2b **Look back at the text. Which of the underlined verbs in the text are modal verbs? Check your answers in the key.**

2c **Circle the correct options to complete the sentences. Use the examples in the text to help you.**

a) A modal verb is followed by an infinitive *with / without* 'to'.

b) Modal verbs do not have singular or plural forms. To use a modal verb in the third person we *add / do not add* 's'.

c) Questions are formed *with / without* the auxiliary verb 'do'.

d) The negative of a modal verb is formed with 'not'; 'not' comes *after / before* the modal verb.

✏ EXAM TASK: Reading (Sentence completion)

3 Read the text from a locksmith's blog. Complete the summary below. Choose **NO MORE THAN TWO WORDS** from the text for each answer.

» Posted by: Giles Swift

People often ask me what skills are necessary to be a good locksmith. As many locksmiths will tell you, locksmiths must be able to work in highly stressful environments. Locksmiths work with the public, so they need good interpersonal skills. They often console clients who are frustrated with their current safety measures. Some customers experience panic when locked out of their homes, businesses or cars. A positive attitude can quickly make your customer feel that he or she needn't be scared.

Strong communication skills are needed. On occasion, a broken component needs replacing and an alternative security measure must be put in place. A locksmith may have to consult manufacturers to ensure this happens.

Locksmiths do not have to obtain an academic degree but they will need to have current expert knowledge of locking devices and electronic alarm systems. As a trainee, and even once you've qualified, you ought to keep up-to-date with new products and developments in security technology.

Customers will recommend a good locksmith and many locksmiths find that they do not need to devote much time to advertising their services. A locksmith should remain professional at all times. Considering a locksmith's work is to open locked doors, a locksmith must not pass on their skills to the general public.

Strong **(1)** .... are necessary as locksmiths often meet customers who are frightened or stressed. The ability to work under **(2)** .... conditions is essential. **(3)** .... qualifications are not necessary, but up-to-date technical **(4)** .... is required. It is advisable to be aware of product developments. It is important for a locksmith always to be **(5)** .... It is vital that they do not teach the **(6)** .... their knowledge.

Grammar tip

We use *be able to* rather than *can* with another modal verb, e.g. *Locksmiths **must** (~~can~~) **be able to** work in highly stressful environments.*

Grammar tip

There are a number of adjectives which are commonly used as an alternative to *must* and *should*, e.g. *crucial, essential, important, necessary, vital.*

Some passive constructions are used too, e.g. *be required, be expected, be allowed.* We use *be supposed to* is used to talk about what people are expected to do and it is often used to imply that expectations were not met, e.g. *A locksmith is supposed to work around 40 hours a week (but they often work more).*

4 Read the Grammar reference and complete the examples with the underlined clauses from the text on page 55.

Grammar reference: *must, have to, should, need*

must or *have to*?

must and *have to* are used to express necessity and obligation; *have to* is more common in conversation than in academic English; *must* is often used to talk about something the speaker feels is necessary, e.g. *As many locksmiths will tell you, you must be able to work in highly stressful environments*; *have to* may indicate that the necessity comes from an outside source, e.g. *A locksmith may have to consult manufacturers.*

- The negative forms have different meanings, e.g.

(1) .... (*must not* = it is wrong to)

(2) .... (*do not have to* = it is not necessary to)

should or *ought to*?

The modal verb *should (not)* is commonly used for giving advice, e.g. *You should contact the MLA for further information*; *ought (not) to* is less common, but is a verb with a similar meaning to *should*,

e.g. **(3)** ....

- *should* can also be used to talk about obligation and duty in a similar way to *must*, but is less strong, e.g. *A locksmith should remain professional at all times.* (= it is expected / important)

need

need behaves as an ordinary verb and is used to say that something is necessary; *need* is most commonly used with

a noun, e.g. **(4)** ....

or followed by the infinitive with *to*, e.g. **(5)** ....

- *need* can also be used as a modal verb and is most common in the negative form *needn't* or *need not*, e.g. *A positive attitude can make your customer feel that they needn't be scared.* (= do not need to)

- When talking about habitual necessity, we prefer *do not need to*, e.g. *Many locksmiths find that they do not need to (needn't) advertise their services.*

Passive forms

- The modal verbs *must* and *should* are followed by *be* + past participle,

e.g. **(6)** ....

- The passive form of *need* is (*need* + *to be* + past participle), but we can also use *need* + *-ing form*,

e.g. **(7)** ....

5 Correct nine errors in the use or choice of *must, should, have to* and *need* in this text on burglary prevention.

You must not leave windows open or unlocked, even if you are only going out for a few minutes. Thieves are opportunists and not need to be given much encouragement to try their luck. Leaving valuables near windows is an open invitation to thieves. If you are going to be away for days or weeks at a time, you will need to take additional action – consider asking your neighbour to close your curtains or park on your drive. You mustn't leave lights on all day. Use a timer device to automatically turn lights and a radio on at night. You should to use a downstairs room with a drawn curtain and sufficient light inside to suggest that the room is occupied. A light doesn't have to be left on solely in the hall – it is not normal for the occupants to spend all night in the hall!

Most of the time security lighting is all that is needed to scare off a potential intruder. But for your house to be secure, you must need to make sure that your physical defences – the locks, the bars and window bolts – will resist attack. All accessible windows must be fitted with key operated locks, unless they are being used as a fire escape. Glass panels in doors should be replace with laminated glass or reinforced with security film or grilles. An internal cover plate needs be fitted to letterboxes. If your flat is on the second floor or above, you need balancing security with fire safety. That means you shouldn't fit your front door with a lock that need a key to open it from the inside.

6 Circle the correct forms in the text about the history of locks. Use the Grammar reference to help you.

Ever since man started to place a value on material possessions, people **(1)** *have needed to keep / ought not to have kept* these possessions secure. However, ancient locks had a basic security problem. Thieves **(2)** *did not need to pick / needn't have picked* the locks since they were made of wood which could be easily chopped or burned.

The Romans were the first civilisation to design metal locks with wards – projections around the keyhole – which meant the lock **(3)** *had to be opened / must be opened* with a proper key.

The basic design of how locks and keys worked remained relatively unchanged for centuries. Evidently, governments **(4)** *should have done / need not have done* more to encourage advances in lock technology since burglaries were common in the rapidly developing cities of the industrial age and false keys were relatively easy to make.

Finally, in 1817, a competition was launched by the UK government to produce an unpickable lock. Jeremiah Chubb developed the first detector lock, which would stop working if an attempt was made to use the wrong key. The owner then **(5)** *had to use / had used* a special key to reset it. In order to test whether the lock was genuinely unpickable, the UK government gave the lock to a convict, who was a locksmith by trade, with the offer of a free pardon if he opened it successfully. The government **(6)** *needn't have had / didn't have to have* any doubts. The Chubb detector lock remained unpicked for another three decades.

Le Serrurier.

Ie fuis Serrurier bien expert
Pour fort bien limer vne clef,
Ce me feroit vn grand meefchef,
Si abufant fuis defcouuert.   ix.

Grammar reference: *must, have to, should, need*

Past use

The past form of *have to* is *had to*; *must* has no past form – we use *had to* instead.

• Use *should have / ought to have* + past participle to talk about past events which did not happen. This use may imply some criticism, e.g. *You shouldn't have left the key outside.*

• *need* is most commonly used as a regular past verb: *needed to*. The negative form in the past *did not need (to)* refers to something that people / organisations did **not** do because it was not necessary, e.g. *In those days, they did not need to lock the door because the area was so safe.*

• *need not have* + past participle is used to refer to something that people / organisations did, although it was not necessary e.g. *You needn't have bought another lock. We could have fixed the old one.*

7 Discuss in small groups.

a) Compare your professions / areas of study. What skills are needed in your professions / studies? For what tasks?

b) Is there anything about your work / study situation that you feel needs changing? Explain why.

c) Think of a situation in your work or studies where things did not go as planned. What was supposed to happen? Who or what was at fault and why?

Eyewitness

1 **Work in pairs and complete this simple memory test.**

How good is your short-term memory?

Look at the list of words below for two minutes. Memorise as many words as you can.

nine	swap	cell	horse	love
plug	rock	apple	table	crawl
army	bank	fire	hold	worm

Now cover the list and see how many words you can write down in two minutes.

Work in pairs. Compare your lists of words. How many did you remember?
The typical storage capacity is between five and nine words. However, it can be surprisingly difficult.

Now do the same experiment with the following words:

horse	tiger	whale	bird	bat
teacher	student	college	homework	test
apple	grape	mango	banana	pear

How many words could you remember this time? Why do you think this is?
Other factors can affect the memorisation of these words too.
What factors can you think of?

2a **Check your grammar!** Underline the examples of *can* and *could* in the instructions for the memory test.

2b **What type of verb are *can* and *could*? What are the grammatical features of these verbs? Think about third person forms, questions, negatives and verbs which follow them.**

2c **Look at the sentences and questions containing *can* and *could* in the memory test again. Discuss the questions in pairs.**

a) Which talk or ask about ability? (Try replacing *can* or *could* with *be / was able to*.)

b) Which are statements that the writer believes to be true?

3a Read the text. Circle the correct options, using the Grammar reference to help you. Sometimes both options are possible.

How often have you gone to find something, been distracted and then **(1)** *have not been able to remember /
have not can remember* what it was you were there for? If you return to your original location, you
(2) *can often remember / can often able to remember* your original intention. The role of context on memory
has been demonstrated in many different ways. In 2007, researchers Mead & Ball **(3)** *could reveal /
succeeded in revealing* a connection between an individual's mood and their ability to recall information.
They played music in a particular key to participants who were studying word lists. When the participants
were asked to recall the word lists, they **(4)** *could remember / managed to remember* significantly more words
if music was playing which was in the same key as at the time of learning. The researchers also found that
the music had altered the participants' feelings. Mood is important in other situations too. Some students
who learn information when they are calm find that they **(5)** *cannot / are not able to* recall information when
they are nervous in the exam room. The reverse may be true for witnesses at crime scenes who
(6) *do not manage to recall / can't recall* events when the fear has subsided.

Grammar reference: modal verbs of ability

- *can (= be able to)* is used to express present ability, and is particularly common with verbs of perception,
  e.g. *feel, hear, see, smell, taste*. It is also common with mental process verbs, e.g. *follow (= understand), guess,
  imagine, picture, remember, understand*, e.g. *How many of the words can you remember?* The negative form is
  can't or *cannot*.

- Future, perfect and infinitive forms use *be able to* in place of *can*, e.g. *When **will** you **be able to** finish the job?*

- *could* is used to express a general ability in the past, but alternatives are used to talk about specific actions in
  the past: *was / were able to, succeeded (+ in + -ing* form*), managed (+ to)*, e.g. *It was only a one-day training course,
  but I was able to / managed to (could) learn plenty.*

  However, it is possible to use *could* to talk about specific actions in the past in the following cases:

  - with the negative forms: *could not, could only, could hardly*, e.g. *He was so ill he could hardly move.*

  - with the verbs of perception and mental process verbs mentioned above, e.g. *We could(n't) smell
    anything unusual.*

3b Work in pairs. Discuss the questions.

a) Do smells and sounds sometimes help you to remember other events?

b) Are you surprised by the scientists' findings? Why / Why not?

✏ EXAM TASK: Speaking (Part 2)

4 Prepare answers to the questions. In pairs, take turns to talk about the topic for one to two minutes.

> Describe a favourite place you went to as a child.
>
> You should say:
>   where the place was
>   what you could see or hear there
>   what you were able to do there
> and explain why you liked it and how it made you feel.

5a **Read the following text. What is an eyewitness?**

Eyewitness testimony is a legal term, referring to an account given by a person (called an eyewitness) of an event they have witnessed. For example, they **(1)** may have seen a road accident or **(2)** may be required to give a description at a trial of a robbery, including identification of criminals and details of the crime scene. In recent years there has been much research into the reasons for the accuracy or otherwise of eyewitness testimony and what **(3)** could be done to improve its reliability.

Generally, juries pay close attention to eyewitness testimony, considering it a reliable source of information. However, research has shown that psychological factors, such as stress and anxiety, **(4)** can affect eyewitness testimony and inevitably, there **(5)** must be an element of anxiety in all eyewitness accounts.

(6) There might be another reason why eyewitness accounts in court are not accurate. An eyewitness's recall of events **(7)** may have been influenced by things that they heard or saw after the crime occurred.

5b **Read the Grammar reference. Then work in pairs. Look at the modal verbs underlined in the text above. Use the Grammar reference to help you explain the writer's choice of the modal verb each time.**

Grammar reference: modal verbs of possibility

Present and future possibility

- *can* is used to talk about events and states that the speaker considers to be true or usually true, *e.g. Even questioning by a lawyer can alter the witness's testimony.*

- *may, might* and *could* are used to speculate and say something is possible in the present or future; *may (not)* and *might (not)* are used to say something is not possible (*could not* is not common in this context), e.g. *He could be nervous. She might not know.*

- *may* is used when there is a slightly greater degree of certainty and is often used in more formal contexts; *might* expresses a lesser degree of certainty.

- *could* is also used to make suggestions of what is possible, e.g. *The government could bring in a new law to give witnesses greater protection. A new law could be brought in to give witnesses greater protection.*

Past possibility and probability

- *may (not) have / might (not) have / could have* + past participle are used to talk about possibility in the past, e.g. *There might have been some flaws in the witness account.* (Note that *could* is not used in the negative here.)

- *must* is used to talk about something that is considered certain or highly probable, based on logical reasoning (deduction); in this context *must* is not used in the negative, *can't / cannot* is used instead, e.g. *It must be false. It can't be true.* The past form is *must have* + past participle; the opposite meaning, i.e. that something is considered highly improbable or impossible, is expressed by *can't / couldn't have* + past participle, e.g. *There must have been a mistake. They can't / couldn't have been present at that time.*

Passive forms

Passive forms to express possibility and deduction are common in academic writing, e.g. *The significance of these results may have been underestimated.*

6 **Read the situations below. Discuss answers to the questions using *may, might, could* or *must*.**

    a) The 60th and 62nd British Prime Ministers of the UK had the same mother and father, but were not brothers. How do you account for this?

    b) A window cleaner is cleaning the windows on the 25th floor of a skyscraper, when he slips and falls. He is not wearing a safety harness and nothing slows his fall, yet he suffered no injuries. How do you explain this?

7 Work in pairs. Read the study and answer the questions using modal verbs of possibility and deduction. Then check the conclusion of the study in the key.

Elizabeth Loftus is one of the leading psychologists in the field of eyewitness testimony. In 1979 she published the results of a study which became known as 'weapon focus'. Participants in this study were left in a waiting area outside a laboratory whilst waiting for the 'real' study to start. While they were waiting, they overheard a discussion in the laboratory about equipment failure, followed by a man leaving the laboratory holding a pen and with grease on his hands.

a) Imagine you are a participant. What do you think when you see the man? Where does he work? What has he been doing?

Participants then overheard a heated discussion in the laboratory with the sound of breaking glass and crashing chairs, followed by a man leaving the laboratory carrying a paper knife covered in blood.

b) Imagine you are a participant. What do you think has happened? Do you think the man is dangerous? Why?

The participants were later asked to identify the men from a set of fifty photographs with the result that 49% correctly identified the man holding the pen, but only 33% could identify the man with the bloodstained knife.

c) What do you think? Why were not many of the participants able to identify the man with the knife?

8 Complete the gaps in this text about another study. Use an appropriate form of the words in brackets each time. More than one answer may be possible.

Yuille & Cutshall (1986) interviewed thirteen witnesses to a real-life shooting in which a storeowner in America was injured and the thief was shot dead. The researchers found that the witnesses closest to the event **(1)** .... (*manage / describe*) it in the most detail and the witnesses that had been the most distressed at the time of the incident **(2)** .... (*able / give*) the most accurate testimony several months later.

The results of this study **(3)** .... (*not / predict*) as they were completely opposite to those that 'weapon focus' would suggest. The witnesses **(4)** .... (*must / experience*) considerable anxiety, yet it does not appear to have negatively affected the eyewitness accounts, nor was their attention overly absorbed by the presence of a weapon. But it **(5)** .... (*be*) that the witnesses had discussed the shooting so often – they **(6)** .... (*even / read*) about the event in the newspapers – that their memories **(7)** .... (*not / be*) entirely their own.

Real world research into eyewitness testimony has a valuable advantage over laboratory research. In laboratory studies, participants are exposed to often unrealistic scenarios presented in an unrealistic way, and **(8)** .... (*may / affect*) by their expectations of the test. Real world events are the only real way to find out how accurately witnesses **(9)** .... (*recall*) events. However, influence on the witnesses from each other, the authorities and media **(10)** .... (*not / control*). Both laboratory and real life studies **(11)** .... (*therefore / provide*) important and contrasting information.

✎ EXAM TASK: Speaking (Part 3)

9 Work in pairs. Discuss the questions.

How might being the witness of any crime affect someone?

Have cities always been dangerous or were they safer in the past?

Could governments do more to control gun crime?

Early warning

1 **Check your grammar!** Read the sentences about natural hazards and answer the questions.

1 Weather forecasters will warn you if wet weather is due.

2 If there is unusually heavy rain in a low-lying area, it results in ....

a) What type of hazard is being referred to?

b) Which grammatical structure(s) are these sentences examples of?

c) These sentences talk about situations which are said to be 'real'. What do you think is meant by the term 'real'?

2 **Match the two parts of the sentences describing natural hazards.**

1 A tropical storm becomes a hurricane

2 If lightning strikes an area of dry vegetation,

3 Meteorologists do not consider a country to be in a heatwave

4 When fine ash and sulphur dioxide from a volcanic eruption reach the atmosphere,

a) it can cause a wild fire.

b) spectacular sunsets are produced.

c) if its winds reach 74 mph.

d) unless temperatures stay 5°C above average for five days.

3 **Work in pairs. Which of the natural hazards in exercise 2 does each sentence talk about / give advice for?**

a) If you live in a high-risk area, clear an area of at least thirty metres around your home.

b) If you have furniture and other outdoor equipment on your patio, you should bring them inside.

c) Provided that you have adequate water, and do not stay in the parked vehicle, you can make journeys by car.

d) If you are visiting a hazard zone, local authorities will supply you with details of evacuation routes.

4 **Look at the sentences in exercise 3. Which of the following do you always find in a first conditional?**

a) the present simple   **b)** if   **c)** will   **d)** a comma

5 **Look at the list of strategies designed to help reduce the impact of the natural disasters in exercise 2. In pairs, discuss ways in which some of these strategies may help.**

urban planning   early warning systems   education   community participation

✎ EXAM TASK: Reading (Identifying information)

6 **Read the text about Cyclone Nargis on page 63. Do the following statements agree with the information given in the text? Write**

TRUE if the statement agrees with the information
FALSE if the statement contradicts the information
NOT GIVEN if there is no information on this

The devastation caused by Cyclone Nargis

1 Disaster relief organisations are predicting further cyclones in Myanmar.

2 Not enough funds have been allocated to disaster prevention worldwide.

3 There was no form of flood early warning system in place in Myanmar in 2008.

4 The weather warnings about Cyclone Nargis did not reach local communities.

5 The roads around the Irrawaddy Delta were in a good state previous to the Cyclone.

6 Computer monitoring of natural hazards is not effective without community involvement.

Global media attention on large-scale disasters such as the Cyclone Nargis in Myanmar in 2008, which claimed at least 130,000 lives and affected over 2 million, has raised the issue of the effectiveness of the humanitarian response to natural hazards. <u>Had a reliable early warning system been in place in Myanmar, could the scale of the disaster have been reduced?</u> Years later, relief agencies are indicating how the humanitarian response would need to change if a similar event happened again.

Regrettably, effective early warning systems are often not an integral part of disaster management, despite evidence of their effectiveness. Flood early warning systems and early action not only save lives but also prevent billions of dollars' worth of damage. It is a fact that if more funds had been invested in disaster risk reduction globally, less would need to be spent on emergency response.

The many lessons learned from Cyclone Nargis serve to remind us of some of the enormous challenges which climate change and socio-economic factors pose for early warning systems. Warnings were issued by the Myanmar Meteorological Service, but did not reach communities. Cyclone Nargis was highly unusual in that it hit from the west, forcing water up the Irrawaddy Delta. Even if the warnings had reached the delta's residents, it was such an exceptional event that many people would not have believed or been prepared to act on the warnings. <u>In addition, their capacity to evacuate the area would have been severely limited by poor roads and infrastructure.</u>

Early warning systems are not just about high-cost, high-technology intervention. In many regions, the warnings captured by satellite monitoring and other technologies would not reach at-risk communities <u>unless a more people-centred approach were in place</u>. The recent success of programmes in Mozambique and Bangladesh, which include allocating response roles to local volunteers and providing skills training for local communities, show us that community-centred early action is crucial.

7 **Read the Grammar reference. Choose examples for each point from the underlined parts of the text in exercise 6. Add them to the Grammar reference.**

Grammar reference: unreal conditions

Some conditionals refer to 'unreal' events or situations, i.e. ones that are imaginary, unlikely or impossible. *Relief agencies are indicating how the humanitarian response* **would need** *to change* **if** *a similar event* **happened** *again.* (if+ past, would + infinitive without *to*) This structure uses past forms but refers to the present or future and is known as a second conditional. *Even* **if** *the warnings* **had reached** *the delta's residents, many people* **would** *not* **have believed** *or* **been prepared** *to act on the warnings.* (if + past perfect, would have + past participle) This is known as a third conditional and refers to the past. (Note that *would have been prepared* is a passive form.)

- Contracted negative forms are common (*hadn't, wouldn't*) in third conditional sentences. Contractions in the affirmative (*had = 'd, would = 'd*) are not common in academic writing.

Conditional sentences do not always follow the same pattern. For example:

- We can leave out *if* from third conditional sentences and invert the subject and *had*,
  e.g. **(1)** .... (formal)
- In the *if*-clause of second conditional sentences we often use *were* instead of *was*,
  e.g. **(2)** ....
- *could* and *might* are commonly used instead of *would* in both forms and are used to sound more tentative,
  e.g. *Could the scale of the disaster have been reduced?*
- *If more funds had been invested in disaster risk reduction globally, less would need to be spent on emergency response.* This sentence combines second and third conditional forms and refers to both the present and the past: *If more funds had been invested* (= refers to a past action), *less would need to be spent* (= refers to a present consequence).
- *If we had more resources, we could have trained more volunteers.* This sentence also combines second and third conditional forms: *If we had more resources* (= existing situation), *we could have trained* (= past consequence).
- *If* does not always appear in a conditional sentence, but is implied,
  e.g. **(3)** ....

8 Use the notes to complete the sentences. Incorporate all the information in the notes. Use both Grammar references in this lesson to help you.

a) *$1 spent on prevention = $4 saved on emergency response*

Evidence suggests that if governments ....

b) *People did not leave their homes. They weren't given enough time.*

If ....

c) *Poverty is severe in this area. People lost their livelihoods in the flood.*

.... less severe in this area if ....

d) *Address the problems: cycle of flood and famine continues.*

The government knew that unless the problems ....

e) *The effects of the cyclone serious – whether early warning system in place or not*

Even .... , ... would have ....

f) *Cyclone took a different path? How much damage caused*

How much .... ?

Grammar reference: real and unreal conditions

Alternatives to *if*

These alternatives are commonly used instead of *if* with a slight difference in meaning:

- *as / so long as,* (first and second conditionals), *provided / providing that, on condition that* (all conditionals) = 'only if' e.g. **Provided that** *you have adequate water, you will be able to make journeys by car.*
- *unless* is used to mean *if … not* (with the idea of 'except if'), e.g. *the warnings would not reach at-risk communities* **unless** *a more people-centred approach were in place* (= except if a more people-centred approach were in place)
- *even if* is used to mean 'whether or not', e.g. *Even if the warning had reached the delta's residents, …*

Grammar tip

In academic writing, the second conditional can be used for considering behaviour, theories and outcomes. The third conditional is frequently used for evaluating ideas or events.

✏ EXAM TASK: Speaking (Part 3)

9 Work in pairs. Discuss the questions. Give examples to support your ideas using structures from this lesson where possible.

What effects does climate change have on global weather patterns?

Who should be responsible for disaster relief?

Some people say there is no such thing as a natural disaster, only natural hazards – what do you think?

Online survey

1a **The text below is about freelance working. In pairs, complete the definitions of words from the text.**

a) A *freelancer* is someone …

b) A *participant* is someone …

c) *Cloud-based computing* is a type of computing …

d) *Customer feedback* is advice …

1b **Check your grammar!** **Complete the sentences.**

a) When we give definitions, we often use a defining relative clause with the relative pronouns **(1)** .... , **(2)** .... or **(3)** ....

b) The relative pronouns **(4)** .... and **(5)** .... can be replaced by *that* in defining relative clauses. However, in academic English, we rarely replace **(6)** .... with *that*.

✎ EXAM TASK: Reading (Matching sentence endings)

2 **Read the text. Complete each sentence with the correct ending, A–F.**

1 There is evidence of	**A**	the loss of a job.
2 Going freelance has been made simpler thanks to	**B**	rising numbers of freelance workers.
3 Many workers go freelance in order to benefit from	**C**	technological developments.
4 Freelance working can be an option after	**D**	participants for the Freelance Industry Report.
5 Social media was used to find	**E**	a less rigid daily routine.
6 The survey was conducted over	**F**	a period of two weeks.

A number of recent surveys conducted into freelance working show that freelancers are fast becoming the new face of the global workforce. Mobile devices and cloud-based computing are becoming increasingly popular, which is making it easier than ever for people to set up on their own. A recent survey in the USA asked respondents, many of whom had chosen to take a freelance career path, the reasons why they were freelancing. 28% wanted to have more flexibility in their schedule. However, 14% had turned to freelancing when made redundant.

Getting a full picture of the scale of the freelance economy is difficult. Any kind of contractor or irregular worker could be considered a freelancer, but might not think of themselves as such. Generally speaking, the freelancers surveyed were highly skilled individuals who worked for themselves but did not employ others. Ed Gandia, who compiled the recent Freelance Industry Report, used a combination of social media and email to find participants for the survey. 1,491 freelancers from around the world took part during the two-week period in which the survey was open.

3a **Look at the sentences from the text and answer the questions about the relative clauses in bold.**

1 *Generally speaking, the freelancers surveyed were highly skilled individuals **who worked for themselves but did not employ others.***

a) If we remove the relative clause, is the definition of freelancers complete? Why / Why not?

2 *1,491 freelancers from around the world took part during the two-week period **in which the survey was open.***

b) If we remove the relative clause, do we have all the information we need? Why / Why not?

3 *Mobile devices and cloud-based computing are becoming increasingly popular, **which is making it easier than ever for people to set up on their own.***

c) If we remove the relative clause, does the sentence still make sense? Why / Why not?

3b Read the Grammar reference and decide which of the relative clauses in exercise 3a are defining and which are non-defining.

Grammar reference: relative clauses

- Defining relative clauses contain information which is essential to the sentence. They are not written between commas, e.g. *A freelancer is someone who works independently.* The relative pronoun *that* can be used instead of *who* or *which*, but is most common in an informal style.

- Non-defining relative clauses contain additional information. They are written between commas. We cannot use *that* as the pronoun in this type of clause, e.g. *Ed Gandia, who compiled the recent Freelance Industry Report, used a combination of social media and email to find participants for the survey.*

- *which* (*and not* what) can also be used to refer to a previous idea or clause, *e.g. Mobile devices and cloud-based computing are becoming increasingly popular, which (what) is making it easier than ever for people to set up on their own.*

- *where* and *when* can be used after nouns referring to time or place and can often be replaced by preposition + *which*, e.g. *the two-week period when / in which the survey was open.* We can use *why* after reason.

4 Add the information in brackets to the sentences describing the charts, adding a relative pronoun as appropriate. Use a comma where necessary.

a) This chart shows where the freelancers are based and the length of their working week. (*responded to the Freelance Industry Report survey*)

b) The graph shows the average hours per week. (*the freelancers worked*)

c) The graph proves that freelancers are hardworking professionals. (*shows the average hours worked every week by region*)

d) One interesting fact is that freelancers in Australia (35%), South America (34%) and Europe (33%) are the most likely to work 40 or more hours per week. (*shatters the myth that people in these regions don't typically work long hours*)

e) Fewer hours were worked by freelancers in North America and Asia. (*people are generally thought to have long working weeks*)

f) The participants answered a range of questions. (*almost half were designers, writers or editors*)

Grammar tip

Use quantity + *of* + *whom / which* to add more information to your sentences when describing a graph, e.g. *A recent survey in the USA asked respondents, many of whom / 28% of whom / a third of whom had chosen to take a freelance career path, the reasons why they were freelancing.*

Graph showing freelancers' average weekly working hours per region.

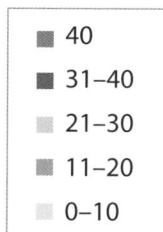

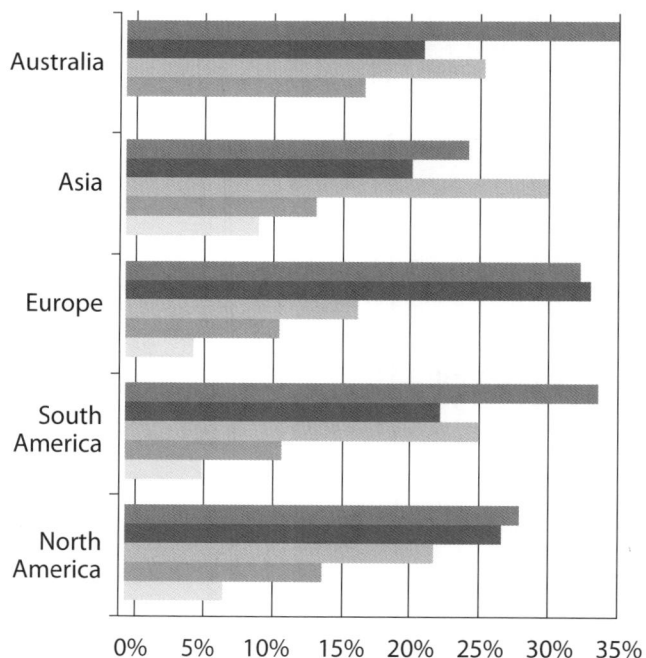

Legend:
- 40
- 31–40
- 21–30
- 11–20
- 0–10

5a **Underline the defining relative clauses in the sentences.**

a) The anonymity that the internet provides makes it the ideal environment for asking customers their opinions about a business, product or service.

b) There are a number of websites where businesses can access software to create a simple online survey.

c) Surveys can be aimed at the general public or there may be a specific group of customers from whom a business wishes to get feedback.

d) There are many different types of questions that are used in a survey.

e) Most people who take part in surveys prefer short multiple-choice questions.

f) Participants don't have to fill in questions which they don't consider relevant to them.

5b **Read the information in the Grammar reference. Delete the words in the sentences in exercise 5a which can be left out. You will need to change the form of one of the verbs.**

Grammar reference: reduced relative clauses

- In defining relative clauses, the relative pronouns *who*, *which* or *that* can often be left out if they are the object of the sentence, e.g. *The freelancer (who) I contacted was not available.*

- We can sometimes leave out the relative pronoun when it refers to the subject if we also leave out part of the verb phrase – so only the participle remains. This is known as a reduced relative clause, e.g. *freelancers* **surveyed** (= who were surveyed); *It is encouraging to see so many new freelancers* **coming** *into the market for the first time* (= who are coming / who come).

Grammar tip

In academic writing, it is unusual to end a relative clause with a preposition. This is often placed before the relative pronouns *which* or *whom*, e.g. *a specific group of customers who a business wishes to get feedback from* > *a specific group of customers from whom a business wishes to get feedback.*

✎ EXAM TASK: Writing (Task 1)

6 **The diagram below shows the stages which are needed to conduct an online survey. Summarise the information by selecting and reporting on the main features. Include at least two relative clauses in your answer.**

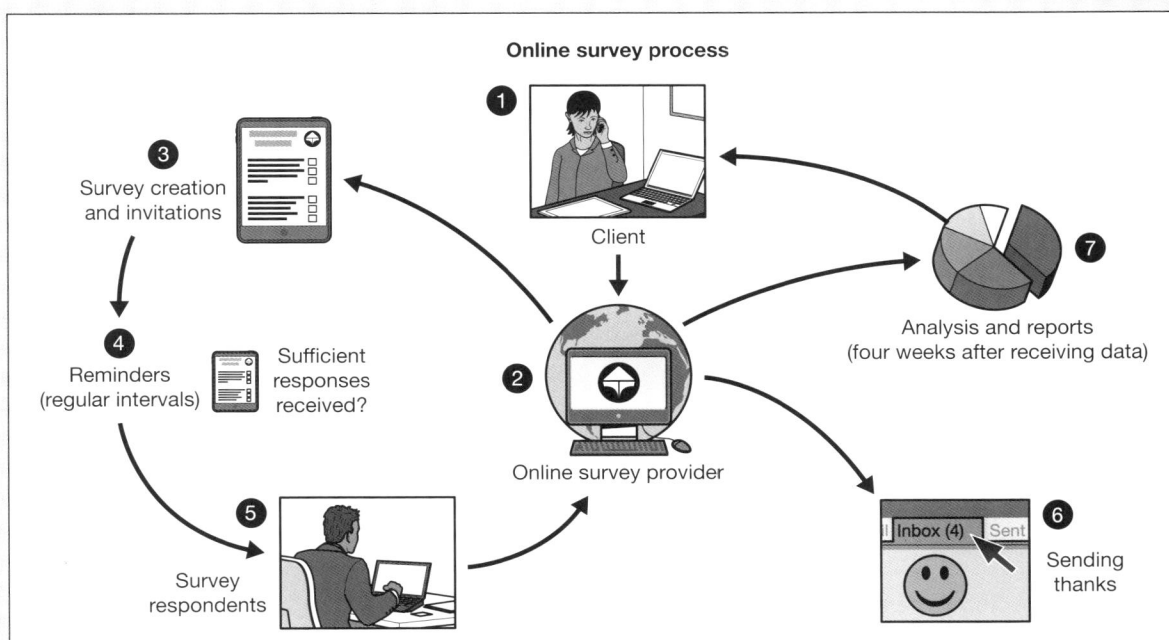

Online survey process

1 Client

2 Online survey provider

3 Survey creation and invitations

4 Reminders (regular intervals)

Sufficient responses received?

5 Survey respondents

6 Sending thanks

7 Analysis and reports (four weeks after receiving data)

Plastic ocean

1 **Work in pairs. How does plastic get into the ocean? Describe what you can see in the diagram. Use the words in the box to help you.**

> drain   marine wildlife   ocean   pipes   plastic bag   river   rubbish bin

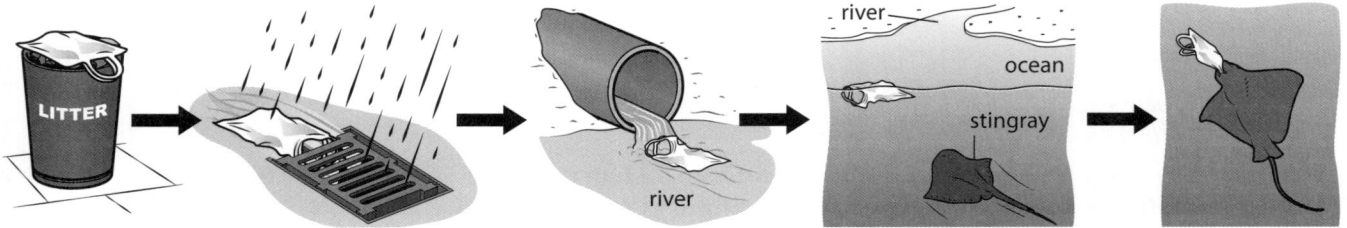

river
ocean
stingray
LITTER
river

2a **Check your grammar!** **Which of these did you use to describe the diagram?**

- active tense, e.g. present simple   ● passive tense, e.g. *is eaten*   ● relative clause, e.g. *A bag which …*

2b **Now read this summary of the same information. Which of the above structures are in this text?**

> A plastic bag **(1)** *which has been left* in a city rubbish bin is blown into a drain. It travels through pipes into a river and from here into the ocean. The plastic is eaten by marine wildlife, **(2)** *which mistake* it for food.

2c **Reduce the words in italics to ONE word only. You will need to change the form of one of the words. What type of words have you used?**

3a **Read the text about plastic pollution. Look at the participle clauses underlined in the text. Complete the rephrases of the clauses.**

> Plastic pollution is a very real and man-made threat to our planet. We produce around 300 million tons of plastic every year, eight million tons of which ends up in the ocean. **(1)** <u>Once discarded</u>, plastic takes a very long time to degrade. **(2)** <u>After breaking down</u> into smaller pieces as a result of the action of UV rays, the plastic litter remains in the sea. These microplastics contain toxic chemicals which, **(3)** <u>when ingested</u>, threaten marine life and ultimately affect human health. In the ocean there are areas where currents converge, **(4)** <u>known as gyres</u>. Marine litter **(5)** <u>accumulating in gyres</u> shows up on satellite images. The most infamous of these is a huge area of floating waste in the Pacific Ocean.
>
> Complete clean-up of our polluted rivers and oceans is a huge challenge, but scientists are researching a range of much-needed solutions to this problem. A team of pioneering scientists have produced a prototype sea vacuum cleaner to pick up surface waste from rivers and oceans. The solar-powered vacuum cleaner is based on the principles of hydro-cyclonic separation, similar to the technique **(6)** <u>used</u> in the bagless vacuum cleaners **(7)** <u>made famous</u> by Sir James Dyson.

1 Once plastic .... , it takes a very long time to degrade.

2 The plastic .... into smaller pieces as a result of UV rays. After that, it remains in the sea.

3 These microplastics contain toxic chemicals, which affect human health when they ....

4 In the ocean there are areas where currents converge, which .... gyres.

5 Marine litter .... in gyres. These show up on satellite images.

6 / 7 The vacuum cleaner uses a technique similar to the one which .... in the bagless vacuum cleaners which .... by Sir James Dyson.

3b **Read the Grammar reference and answer the questions below. Find examples in the text in exercise 3a.**

Grammar reference: participles and participle clauses

Participle clauses can make your writing more succinct and less repetitive.

- Participles can be used like adjectives. *-ing* participles are similar to active verbs, e.g. *floating waste* (= *waste which floats*); *-ed* participles usually have a passive meaning, e.g. *polluted river* (= *a river which has been polluted*).

- Participles can combine with other words into participle clauses. (When used after nouns, these are similar to reduced relative clauses.) Use the *-ing* participle as an alternative to the active form of a verb when the subject is the same in each clause, e.g. *It's an example of marine litter **accumulating** in a gyre.* Use the *-ed* participle as an alternative to the passive form of a verb, e.g. *the vacuum cleaners* (*which have been*) *made famous by Sir James Dyson.*

- *-ing* participle clauses are common with the conjunctions and prepositions *after, before, on, since, when, while, without*, e.g. *After breaking down into smaller pieces …*

- We can use *-ed* participle clauses after *if, when, once, until*, e.g. *Once discarded, … .*

a) How can including participle clauses improve your writing?

b) Which examples of participles used as adjectives does the reference provide? What others can you find in the text? (The term '-ed forms' includes regular and irregular participles, so *polluted* and *left* are both examples of *-ed* forms.)

c) In participle clauses, what are the *-ing* and *-ed* participle forms used as an alternative to?

d) How many examples of participles following conjunctions and prepositions can you find in the text?

4 **Look at the sentences about research into bacteria which can degrade one type of plastic. Combine each pair of sentences to make one sentence using a participle clause. You may need to leave out one or two words from the original sentences.**

a) A new species of bacteria is able to consume PET, one of the world's most common plastics. / It has been discovered by Japanese scientists.

b) PET is both lightweight and strong. / It is widely used to make disposable water bottles.

c) The discovery could be a breakthrough in managing the plastic. / The discovery was published in the journal *Science.*

d) Scientists collected 250 PET-contaminated samples from a plastic bottle recycling site. / The samples included sediment, soil and wastewater.

e) Scientists screened the microbes which were living on the samples. / They found just one of the bacteria species, which is named *Ideonella sakaiensis*, was responsible for PET degradation.

f) Further tests revealed the bacteria used enzymes to break down the PET. / This generated an intermediate chemical.

g) The chemical was then taken up by the cell, where it was broken down even further by other enzymes. / This provides the bacteria with carbon and energy to grow.

h) A community of *Ideonella sakaiensis* could break down a thin film of PET in just six weeks. / This happens if it is kept at a temperature of 29°C.

Grammar tip

Some verbs which are not often used in the continuous form are common in an *-ing* clause, e.g. *consisting of, containing, including, involving, providing, requiring, resembling.*

5 **Read the sentences describing how the proposed sea vacuum cleaner works. Circle the correct options.**

The diagram shows how dirty water is cleaned through the process of hydro-cyclonic separation.

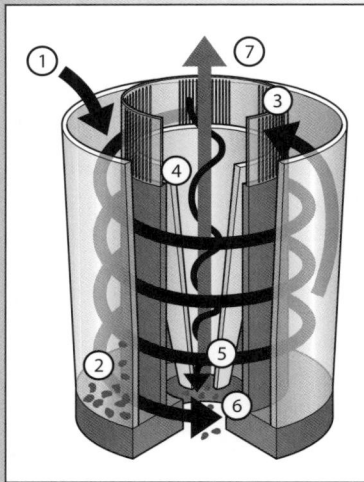

1 First dirty water is drawn in by a pump. This water goes into the top corner of a bin. The water spirals around, *creates / creating* centrifugal force*.

2 The force causes the larger plastic particles to spin out of the water stream and *fall / falling* to the bottom of the bin.

3 The water then flows through a filter, which *catches / catching* more plastic particles.

4 After this, the water continues through a conical cylinder *housed / housing* in the bin.

5 The sloping walls of the cylinder cause the water *contains / containing* the smallest plastic particles to spin down to the bottom of the cone at an increasing speed.

6 Centrifugal force (6) *acts / acting* on the water stream increases, *forces / forcing* the plastic particles against the sides of the cone.

7 The plastic particles fall through the hole in the bottom of the cone, while the water *escapes / escaping* up the centre.

centrifugal force = a force which causes an object moving in a circular path to move away from the centre of its path.

Grammar tip

- We can use *-ing* participle clauses to talk about simultaneous actions or states.
- When it is used at the start of a sentence, a participle clause is followed by a comma.

✎ EXAM TASK: Writing (Task 1)

6 **The diagram below shows the stages in the recycling of plastic bottles. Summarise the information by selecting and reporting the main features. Include at least two participle clauses in your answer.**

Recycling plastic bottles

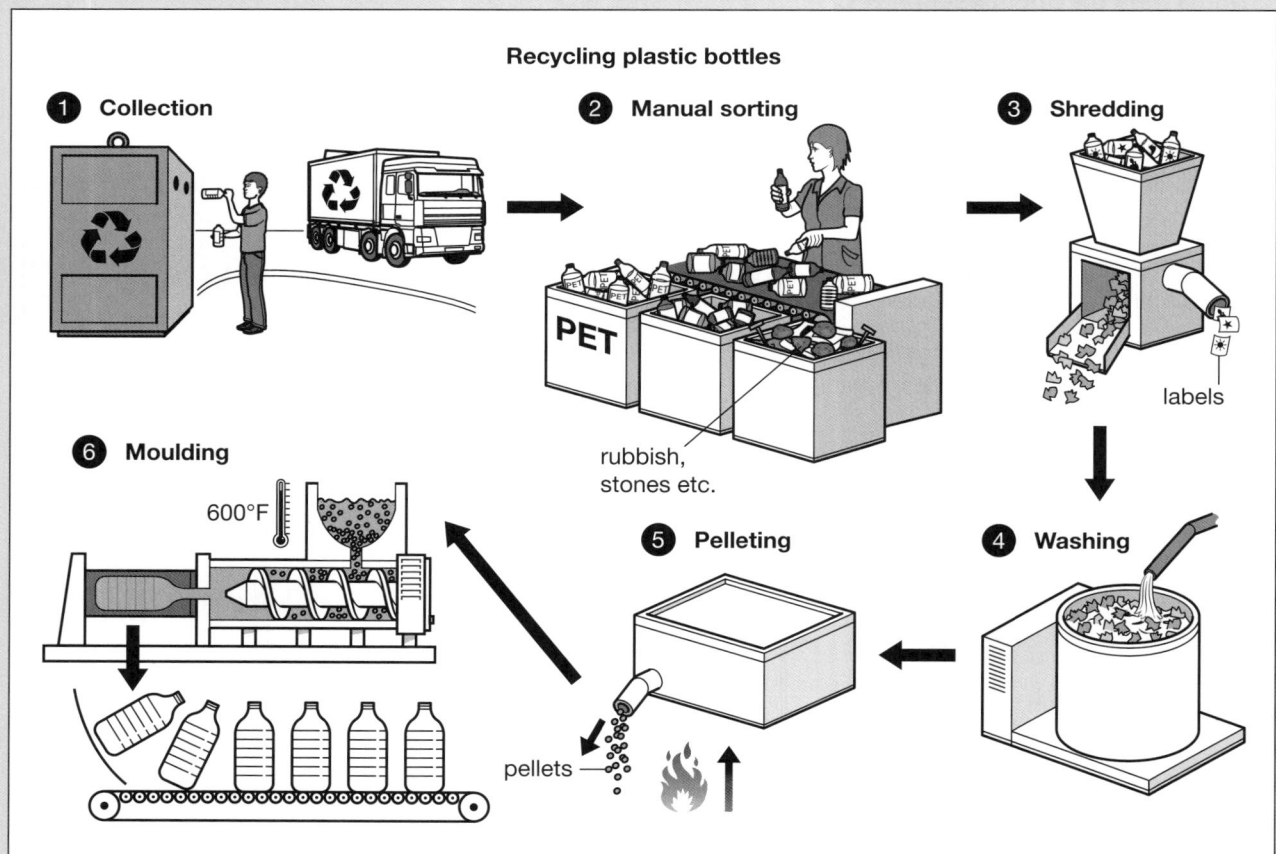

1 Collection

2 Manual sorting

PET

rubbish, stones etc.

3 Shredding

labels

6 Moulding

600°F

5 Pelleting

pellets

4 Washing

Answers

The evolution of cephalopods (pages 6–9)

1a Students' own answers.

1b a and c are true: cephalopods are invertebrates and some species (especially squid, octopus and cuttlefish) are intelligent.
b and d are not true: cephalopods are not endangered and they have short lifespans.

2 **1** appears **2** have been rising **3** seems **4** are now investigating **5** is changing

3 **a** continuous **b** ongoing, temporary **c** state, an unchanging state

4 **a)** Use of senses **b)** Preferences and feelings **c)** Description **d)** Mental process verbs **e)** Possession

5 **1** resemble **2** consists **3** have **4** is thinking **5** sounds **6** does not always mean **7** is looking **8** how do they know **9** contains **10** appears **11** see / can see **12** like **13** are gradually realising **14** recognise **15** represent **16** differs **17** is currently challenging **18** including

6 **a** Students' own answers.
b We consider that intelligent animals have evolved, like humans, partly as a result of long and social lives, but cephalopods have short lifespans and are not sociable.
c Students' own answers.

7 **Sample answer**
Animals have always been used as a food source and are also often exploited for the testing of medicine and products which are for human use. However, *some people now feel that* this is not acceptable.
The fact that humans have canine teeth is enough to convince many people that we are carnivores and it is natural for us to eat meat. For this reason, *many people believe that* the farming of animals is acceptable. Since the consumption of animals ensures our survival, then it is not surprising that *people also assume that* medicines which will be used to treat humans will first be tested on animals.
However, the large-scale production of meat is something that I do not believe is natural. We are now aware that humans can get adequate nutrition, *including protein*, from other food sources. *It appears that* better education is needed on the alternatives to meat. Some of the medical testing that is done on animals is not essential and a considerable amount of unnecessary testing is still done for cosmetics. *It seems likely that* animals suffer pain and loss in much the same way as humans. *This means that* keeping them in laboratories is unacceptable. *Current research into the lives of marine animals is leading us to question* our assumptions about animals. Studies on octopus and squid, for example, show that they are far more intelligent than many of us realise and deserve our respect.
To conclude, while *I recognise that* humans will want to consume meat, the current extent of meat production is unnecessary. We should educate people on the benefits of meat-free diets and the testing of non-essential products on animals should be banned. This would go some way towards improving the rights of animals.

8 Students' own answers.

Information overload (pages 10–12)

1a Students' own answers.

1b **a** 1 **b** 4 **c** 3 **d** 2

2a **a)** increase; (also possible: rise)
b) report; (some other options are: survey, researcher)
c) this year; (some other options are: today, this month, this week)
d) a day; (also possible: every day)
e) for decades; (some other options are: for ages, for years)
f) online; (also possible: internet, cyber)

2b **a)** present perfect simple (*has been*), present simple (*spend*)
b) present perfect simple (*has found*), present simple (*admits, spend*)
c) past simple (*commissioned*)
d) present simple (*checks*)
e) present perfect continuous (*have been warning*)
f) present continuous (*are starting*)

3 **1** leads up to now **2** give news of recent events **3** may be understood or implied **4** recent studies **5** with questions beginning *How long?* **6** present perfect continuous **7** which the speaker views as more long-term

4 **1** has been increasing **2** has not brought **3** have set up **4** has suggested / suggests **5** has demonstrated / demonstrates **6** have been published **7** appeared **8** have been complaining **9** worried **10** constantly puts / is constantly putting **11** have discovered **12** has been monitoring **13** has shown / shows **14** has proved / proves

5 Students' own answers.

6 **1** I've recently started / I recently started **2** I've become **3** I celebrated **4** I've been feeling / I felt **5** advised **6** have grown up **7** I turned off **8** Have I missed **9** I've installed / I installed **10** I've reduced / I reduced **11** has already given **12** I've been sleeping **13** I haven't woken up **14** I've come / I came **15** I've never thought

7&8 Students' own answers.

A dream come true (pages 13–15)

1a **a)** The Wright Brothers made the first powered flight in an aeroplane.
b) Alberto Santos-Dumont made the first flight of a powered aeroplane in Europe.
c) Amelia Earhart was the first female pilot to fly across the Atlantic.
d) Wiley Post made the first solo flight around the world.
e) Frank Whittle invented the jet engine.

1b the past simple, e.g. *made, flew*; the past perfect, e.g. *had made, had told*; the past continuous, e.g. *were achieving, was attempting*
a) had made, achieved
b) had built, (had) flown, carried out
c) disappeared, was attempting
d) made, became
e) told, had come up with

2 **1** False **2** False **3** Not Given **4** False **5** True **6** True

3 **a)** 3 **b)** 1 **c)** 2

4 **1** was flying **2** had been wearing **3** had received **4** had become

5 **1** had been watching **2** had built **3** started **4** had been working **5** drove **6** had to **7** crossed **8** had been watching / were watching **9** had won **10** refused **11** had reached **12** had been / was **13** had been changed **14** was never told / had never been told **15** had been awarded **16** became **17** received / had received **18** charmed

6 Students' own answers.

The future of schooling (pages 16–18)

1 Students' own answers.

2a I'm studying pharmacy. As part of the course, I'm going to do a placement with a pharmaceutical company. It starts in the summer.
I come to the library to study most days. When I finish my studies, I might take some time out to travel. I'm taking the IELTS exam next week. I hope my test score will improve my chances of getting a job in another country.

2b There are five different forms used to talk about the future in exercise 2a: *be going to, present simple, present continuous, will, might*.

● *It's going to start* could be used instead of *It starts*. The present simple is common for describing schedules and timetables; *be going to* is most often used for plans. *Be going to* could be used here as there is a plan for the placement to go ahead in the summer.
● *I'm taking* could be replaced by *be going to take*. The present continuous is often used when something has been arranged: the student has applied to take the exam and has a test date. *Be going to* could be used as the student is planning to take the exam.
● *be going to improve* could be used instead of *will improve*. Both *will* and *be going to* are used for predictions of future events; *will* is more common after verbs talking about what we think or reckon will happen, such as *think* or *hope*.
● *be going to take* could be used instead of *might take* but this changes the meaning. *be going to take* means that the student intends to travel; *might* shows that this is a possibility the student is considering. (NB *will* is a modal verb. Other modal verbs are also often used with a future meaning, e.g. *I might / may change jobs*.)

3a **a)** In Text A, questions raised are: how will the digital competence of young people affect classroom practice? How will young people navigate the vast amount of information that is available?
In Text B we find out that Salman Khan used to be a financial analyst. Now he runs an educational organisation.

3b **b)** We are on the verge of a truly digital age. / By the end of the decade the whole world will have learnt how to access information online. / The classroom will be flipped. / In ten or twenty years all US students will be following a similar model. Technology will be used to perform a number of common duties, such as generating tests.

4 **1** In ten or twenty years all US students will be following a similar learning model
2 By the end of the decade, the whole world will have learnt how to access information online.
3 In the same time period, technology will become (~~will be becoming~~) essential for performing a number of common duties, such as generating tests.
4 He had no idea where it would lead.
5 We are on the verge of a truly global digital age.
6 The future classroom will be flipped.

5 **1** going to learn **2** Both are possible. **3** was to **4** Both are possible. **5** will not be able to **6** will be **7** Both are possible. (In the original quote, Mitra used 'shall'.) **8** will have become **9** Both are possible. **10** will be learning **11** will have faded away **12** will be replaced

6 Students' own answers.

7 **Sample answer**
Some people argue that teachers can never be replaced by computers, whereas others consider that computers will one day take over human jobs, including the role of the teacher. Technology is already being used extensively in classrooms. Teachers have interactive whiteboards and are able to make use of video to explain new topics in a more engaging way. In the future teachers will be able to make greater use of software to assess students' performance as well as carry out tasks such as generating tests. In this way, technology will be a tool to help teachers rather than an alternative to the teachers themselves.
Children and learners will always be motivated by an inspiring teacher. In the classroom of the future the teacher will still be necessary, but their role will have changed. Teachers are almost certain to spend less time on formal teaching, and can dedicate their time to helping students practise new concepts instead. Data interpretation and collaborative working are likely to become core skills which teachers will be able to help develop. They might also be able to guide students in the choice of material for their level. In short, technology will allow the teacher to spend more time encouraging students.
In education, as in many other areas, we need to adapt to new ways of working. In twenty years' time, teachers will still be playing a central role in our education. We have nothing to fear from developments in technology. On the contrary the future for education looks very promising.

Toxic footprint (pages 19– 21)

1 **a)** Students' own answers.
b) In weaving, it is important to prevent the yarn from breaking so chemicals are added to strengthen the yarn and reduce friction.

2 **1** are soaked **2** are shredded **3** are dried **4** are combined, turns … into **5** is soaked, looks **6** is filtered, (is) stored

3 passive

4 **1** (the) spinneret **2** (the) godet wheels **3** (the) spinning cylinder / Topham box

5 **1** *can be given, could be used*
2 *must then be washed*
3 *ready to be spun*
4 *After being bathed, Before being woven.*

PHOTOCOPIABLE

6 **a) 1** past continuous *(was being threatened)* **2** past simple *(was found)* **3** modal + passive *(could be produced)*
b) Suggested answer: *In the 1860s a disease which affected the silkworm was threatening the French silk industry.* The subject *'a disease which affected the silkworm'* is rather heavy. For reasons of style, longer or weighty expressions can be put at the end of a clause.
c) By putting the disease at the start of the sentence, it follows on better from the previous sentence. This is a question of writing style, and it is quite common to begin a sentence with a topic that is known about, leaving new information to the end of the sentence.
d) The passive can be used to avoid repetition of the subject. Suggested answer: *The first factory was built shortly after.*
e) Some verbs are not used in the passive tense. These include some state verbs, such as *become, have, seem* and intransitive verbs (verbs which have no object) e.g. *appear, arrive, come, die, go, remain, sit, sleep, wait.* Suggested answer: *Early artificial silk was highly flammable and more stable versions of the material (or rayon) were subsequently developed (developed subsequently* is also possible).

7 **a)** The toxic footprint of textiles has become a serious environmental and health issue.
b) Both workers and consumers risk being affected by the chemicals that are used at each textile processing stage.
c) Some finishing treatments, such as water resistance, have been shown to have hazardous properties.
d) Consumers are likely to be exposed to chemicals by inhaling fibre dust from a textile.
e) Besides being linked to a range of health issues, some chemicals from clothing accumulate in the environment.
f) The fashion industry seems to have an enormous impact on the environment.
g) Manufacturers are not expected to list chemicals on garment labels.
h) The Global Organic Textile Standard (GOTS) is considered to be one of the world's leading processing standards for textiles.
i) The GOTS logo may (only) be displayed (only) on clothes which meet certain environmental standards.
j) The chemicals in all the processing stages of a garment must meet environmental criteria.

8 Students' own answers.

Infographics (pages 22– 24)

1 Students' own answers.

2 Suggested answers: **a)** People often like infographics because they are accessible. The information is presented simply and clearly and is easier to recall.
b) They have become popular because of the large amounts of data we now receive and because computers can analyse the data more easily.

3 **a)** Uncountable nouns in the texts are: *data, information, education, journalism, marketing, technology, memory, information, knowledge, content, browsing, news.*
Note: the use of *data* is controversial. Strictly speaking, *data* is the plural of the Latin *datum*. However, the contemporary use of *data* is as an uncountable noun similar to *information*.
b) singular, e.g. *Technology feeds a global demand, Information is a collection*
c) singular or plural, e.g. *Infographics are, Our brains have, An information graphic is*

d) Yes, sometimes, e.g. *economics, the news.* Some other examples of this are: *linguistics, mathematics, physics, politics, athletics, gymnastics, measles.*

4 **a)** *Infographics are often used in education*: education (uncountable) refers to the process of teaching and learning.
b) *Every child deserves the chance of an education*: an education (countable) refers to the knowledge that an individual gets from attending school.

5 **1** amount of **2** Some **3** little of **4** How much **5** much of **6** many of

6 Students' own answers.

7 **1** some **2** several **3** all **4** a few **5** many **6** amount **7** number **8** None **9** significant proportion **10** little **11** a few **12** enough

8a **Sample answer**
This chart shows the number of people who attended cultural events and places of culture in Scotland in 2014. A large proportion of people went to the cinema – over half of the participants in the survey. Other popular events were live music, theatre or visits to museums –around a third of people attended each of these. Many people (around one fifth) stated they went to an arts exhibition. A similar number were present at street arts events. There were fewer people attending the other events. Comparatively few people (11%) spent time at a dance show and a small number of respondents frequented a classical music performance. A small fraction of those surveyed went to a reading group. 20% of the participants stated they went to none of the events during the course of the year.

8b **Suggested answer:**
Bar charts are useful because they are simple to create and easy to interpret. If a bar chart contains too much information, it can be complicated to read. Bar charts take up a large amount of space on the page so information to include in a bar chart needs to be carefully selected.

Pictures of the floating world (pages 25–27)

1 Students' own answers.

2a Text A is missing definite articles *(the)* and indefinite articles *(a/an)*.

2b In 1831, at **the** peak of his long career, Hokusai produced **a** series of woodblock prints, entitled *Rare Views of Japanese Bridges*. **The** series depicts scenes of daily life on and around bridges in Japan. In *Tenma Bridge in Setsu Province*, **a** fleet of ships passes beneath **a** curved bridge. People crowd **the** bridge to watch **the** ships.

3 single countable nouns: *bridge, whale*; plural countable nouns: *people, ships*; uncountable nouns: *daily life, water*

	a/ an	the	∅
Singular countable nouns	✔	✔	✗
Plural countable nouns	✗	✔	✔
Uncountable nouns	✗	✔	✔

4a They liked his use of perspective (the flattening of space) as well as the recurrent themes of nature and daily life.

4b 1 When the prints … 2 the images of well-known characters which were featured in earlier Japanese prints 3 & 4 the world, the sea 5 the first time 6 A print (often known as *The Great Wave*) 7 a craze (for collecting Japanese art) 8 & 9 Traders, nature 10 Europe 11 Western artists 12 the poor

5 1 An 2 the 3 the 4 Ø 5 a 6 a 7 A 8 Ø 9 Ø 10 Ø 11 The 12 the 13 the 14 the 15 the 16 Ø 17 a 18 The

6 **Sample answer:**
In traditional woodblock printing, the artist first draws the design on paper. The 'key block' is created by pasting the paper design onto a woodblock, usually made of cherry wood. The artist then follows the drawing, using a number of different chisels to transfer the image onto the surface of the woodblock.

Ink is applied to the surface of the woodblock with a brush and then a sheet of paper is placed on top. Rubbing a circular pad over the back of the piece of paper presses the ink on to the paper. The round pad is known as a 'baren' and is traditionally made of a flat coil of straw or bamboo fibre.

The print is laid out to dry for five minutes on mats next to a window which is slightly open. It is then flattened between sheets of heavy card. One or two hours later the finished print is ready. Using this process, an artist can make multiple copies of each work.

7 Students' own answers.

Selfish society (pages 28–30)

1a 1 We 2 No one 3 anything 4 yourself 5 someone 6 none 7 every, anything, yourself, no one, we, someone and none are pronouns. Pronouns are words that can be used to replace a noun or noun phrase; *every* is a determiner. Determiners come before a noun (but are not adjectives). Other common determiners are *a*, *the*, *this*, *that*, *his*, *her*, *some*, *many*.

1b Students' own answers

2 **a)** *each other* and *one another* are possible here. The reciprocal pronouns: *each other* and *one another* mean the same and are used with a plural subject when the action is reciprocal; *love ourselves* means each person loving and looking after his or her own self.
b) *every* or *each* would be possible here as they are generally used with singular countable nouns. *every* has a meaning which is similar to *all*, e.g. *every opportunity or all opportunities*; *each* is used when the speaker wants to put the emphasis on separate people or things, *each opportunity* has the meaning of 'each separate opportunity'.
c) *none* or *not any* are possible here and mean the same; *not any* is not normally used as the subject of a sentence. You can use *none* instead, e.g. *The hotel is busy. None* ~~Not any~~ *of the rooms are free. Neither* is used to talk about two people or things and means 'not one or the other', e.g. *Do you prefer tea or coffee? (I drink) neither.*
d) Both are possible. There is no real difference in meaning between *no one / nobody* or *someone / somebody* etc.
e) Both options are possible with differences in meaning: *him* could be, for example, Tom's son, brother, father or friend, whereas *himself* refers to Tom.

3a 1 e 2 f 3 g 4 i 5 d 6 b 7 c 8 a 9 h
3b Students' own answers.

4 **a)** 3 **b)** 9 **c)** 2 **d)** 8 **e)** 6 **f)** 1 **g)** 5 **h)** 4 **i)** 7

5 Students' own answers.

6 1 each other 2 all of us 3 none 4 anyone 5 their It would be unusual to refer to a student as *he / his* here, since we don't know or need to mention if the student is male or female. 6 them 7 either 8 all 9 something useful

7 **Suggested answer:**
To conclude, human beings are by nature social and that means we care about <u>each other</u>. It is not humans that have changed, but technology. <u>All of us</u> are having to adapt to the fast pace of technological change and find new ways to make a difference. Young people have already found that the power of social media can be used to promote good causes. This proves that we are not becoming a selfish society and that we will always look for <u>something</u> we can do to help others.

Global learning (pages 31–33)

1 Students' own answers.

2 1 It 2 this conclusion 3 It ('The study' would also be possible.) 4 These findings ('These results' would also be possible.)

3a Students' own answers.

3b 1 It is important to encourage a child's desire to read independently.
2&3 It is likely that a strong reading ability enables children to absorb and understand new information (not ~~That a strong reading ability enables children to absorb new information is likely~~); it is clear how crucial it is to provide access to a wide range of books (not ~~How crucial it is to provide access to a wide range of books is clear.~~)
4 there is thought to be a link between improving literacy levels and the availability of mobile devices
5 There seems to be a tendency
6 these findings show
7 that argument does not take into account

4 **a) 1 It is completely unacceptable that** a fifth of all children in England, and close to a third of disadvantaged children, are unable to read well when they leave primary school. **2 This situation** creates obstacles to a fairer society. **3** It is not just impossible **for these children to** experience the joy of reading. **4 It is also more likely to** prevent poorer children from achieving their potential in secondary school and beyond.
b) 1 There are believed to be over 750 million adults worldwide who are illiterate. **2** Roughly two-thirds **of those who cannot read or write** are female. **3 It is often claimed that** population growth has caused this global literacy crisis. **4** However, **it is probable that** underinvestment in adult literacy programmes in communities and workplaces is also to blame.
c) 1 Of the 650 million primary school age children in the world, **it is thought that** 250 million are not learning basic literacy skills. **2** However, **it must be** remembered that tremendous progress has been made in some countries. **3** An estimated 17 million more children are now learning the basics at school in sub-Saharan Africa – **this is** due in part to the abolition of school fees. **4 This figure** represents an impressive 45% more children learning at schools.
d) 1 It is becoming more and more evident **how important** mobile technology could be for literacy development. **2 It seems that** hundreds of thousands of people in countries like Ethiopia, Nigeria and Pakistan are reading more now that they can read on their mobile phones. **3** A survey conducted by UNESCO reveals that **this trend** was more pronounced among women than men.

4 It is also significant that one in three mobile readers are reading to their children from their phones.
5 These examples highlight the potential of mobile technology for literacy programmes.

5 Students' own answers.

6 **Sample answer**
Many children come from homes where reading is actively encouraged. However, <u>this</u> should not only be the responsibility of parents. By supporting young people in their reading, schools are encouraging a lifelong interest in learning.
Reading is an essential skill. By making sure children have a variety of books to choose from and by reading themselves, <u>it is possible for parents to encourage this</u> in children from an early age. Children whose parents read with them on a regular basis usually enjoy reading and make the most progress. In contrast, some children lose interest if their parents do not encourage them. <u>It must be remembered</u> that some parents lack confidence in reading themselves or do not have adequate time available.
However, reading is not about enjoyment alone. <u>It has been suggested that</u> reading ability can impact on all learning and can therefore influence a child's success at school and beyond. It is the responsibility of schools to ensure that children are given access to a wide range of reading material. <u>It is also important that</u> schools give <u>those who</u> struggle with reading adequate time to make progress in <u>this fundamental skill</u>. Governments should prioritise provision for reading and make sure that no child leaves primary school without being able to read.
<u>It is unacceptable that</u> any child in today's world should leave school without the skills required to make a success of their lives. Parents, governments and schools should work together to make reading a priority for all children.

A more nutritious snack (pages 34–36)

1a Students' own answers.
1b **1** higher **2** more likely **3** as / so adventurous **4** less hard **5** the most well-known **6** more easily **7** healthier

2 **a)** False (Insect farming takes up less living space.)
b) True
c) False (Three insects have a much higher nutritional value.)
d) False (They were by far the highest.)
e) True
f) False (This is true in only some situations.)

3a **a)** *far*, *even*, *significantly*, *slightly*, *much*, *just*, *considerably* modify comparatives, *by far* modifies superlatives
b) All the words except *slightly* and *just* suggest that there is a strong degree of difference between the two types of farming.

3b Students' own answers.

4 **a)** more than twice as many, as
b) far fewer, than
c) marginally higher than
d) similar to those from
e) Easily the most

5a X is calcium
5b **Suggested answers:**
There is three times as much sodium in beef as in silkworm, but beef contains less calcium.

The levels of iron and calcium in crickets are by far the highest. Unfortunately the level of sodium is quite the highest too.

The protein content in crickets is about the same as in beef. The level of protein in silkworms is the least at 14.8g.

The most nutritious food source is a topic for debate. In terms of protein, iron and calcium, crickets are the most nutritious food source. Unfortunately, they contain a much higher quantity of sodium. Beef is high in protein but is also high in sodium. Levels of calcium and iron in beef are comparatively low. The level of calcium in silkworm is the highest, but protein content is slightly lower.

6 **Sample answer:**
The charts show the greenhouse gas production, energy use and land use required to produce 1 kg of protein from mealworms, milk and beef.
Beef production produces 170 kilos equivalent of carbon dioxide. This is significantly higher than the greenhouse gases emitted by the other forms of protein. The amount of CO_2 produced by mealworm production for a similar quantity of protein is by far the smallest.
The energy use for mealworm production is about the same as for milk. Beef production uses almost twice as much energy. For land use, the figures are even more surprising. Land use for beef production is considerably greater and is more than the land use for mealworms and milk combined. Mealworm production uses far less land: only 20 m^2 is needed to produce 1 kg of protein.
On the basis of this study, mealworms are a more environmentally-friendly source of animal protein than either milk or beef.

The habit loop (pages 37–39)

1 **1** The prefrontal cortex
2 decisions
3 (an) automatic routine
4 basal ganglia

2 & 3

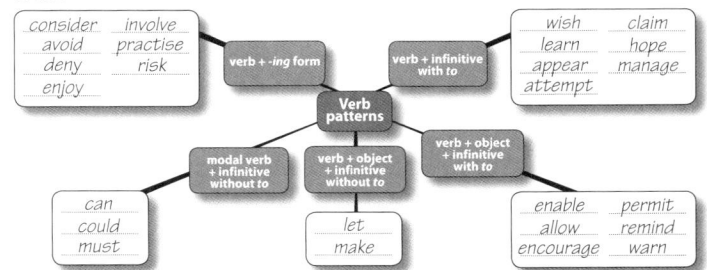

4 **1** to be able **2** ease **3** to remember **4** to quit **5** diagnosing **6** to find out **7** making **8** feel **9** to follow **10** to change

5 **1** deny **2** repeating **3** acknowledged **4** biting **5** notice **6** using **7** walking **8** to make **9** appears

6 & 7 Students' own answers.

The container revolution
(pages 40–42)

1   **a)** freight **b)** cargo **c)** a transport network **d)** a shipping container

2   The text compares sea, air and rail freight. Road freight is also mentioned.
Benefits ...
of sea: cheaper (plenty of cargo space), recently reduced fuel consumption / carbon dioxide emissions; ... of air: faster, less damage to goods; ... of rail: low carbon dioxide emissions, useful for countries with common borders.
Drawbacks ...
of sea: slower; ... of air: expensive (limited cargo space).

3   **a)** world trade = trade which is carried out across the world
sailing speed = the speed at which a boat sails
key argument = the argument which is key / most important
air freight = all freight which is carried by air
cargo ship = a type of ship which carries cargo
road transport = all transport which is done by road
rail freight network = the system of routes on which rail freight is carried
b) They are all nouns. Most are nouns formed of two words, usually two nouns. In the example *sailing speed, sailing* is a noun formed from a verb; in the example *key argument, key* is an adjective.
c) Plural forms are: *world trade* (uncountable), *sailing speeds, key arguments, air freight* (uncountable), *cargo ships, road transport* (uncountable), *rail freight networks*
The second word is changed to form the plural, e.g. *cargo ship > cargo ships.*

4   1 E 2 C 3 B 4 G 5 D

5a   1 a tremendous boom 2 increasingly globalised markets 3 increasing demand 4 transport entrepreneur 5 people around the world 6 truck trailers with cargo inside 7 improvement(s) in 8 McLean's idea that containers could be moved seamlessly between ships, trucks and trains
5b   A – G are all noun phrases.

6   1 Ocean shipping (not ~~Oceans shipping~~)
2 iron ore (not ~~iron's ore~~)
3 The drawback of container shipping (not ~~Container shipping's drawback~~)
4 port facilities with special cranes, storage space and railway systems (not ~~port facilities have special cranes~~ ...)
5 a relatively small number (not ~~a relative small number~~)
6 the ports of Europe and East Asia (not ~~Europe and East Asia's ports~~)
7 in thirty years' time (not ~~in the time of thirty years~~)
8 innovations in design (not ~~innovate in design~~)
9 fuel consumption (not ~~fuel's consumption~~)
10 The problem of what to do with returning vessels is (not ~~The problem that what to do with returning vessels is~~)
11 mineral resources (not ~~minerals resources~~)
12 the costs of (not ~~the costs to~~)

7   **Sample answer**
The line graph shows the growth in international ocean freight of oil and gas, containerised dry cargo and the principal types of bulk cargo (iron ore, coal, grain, phosphates and bauxite) between the years of 1980 and 2014.
There has been a dramatic increase in ocean freight during this time in line with the upward trend in world trade. A slight dip in the quantities of oil and gas transported at the beginning of the 1980s is balanced out by a steady rise in the following years. The amount of oil and gas carried has increased by about a third in the 34-year period. An increasing amount of bulk cargo is transported worldwide. 3,112 tonnes were transported in 2014 compared with 608 tonnes in 1980. The transportation of containerised dry cargo is on the increase. In 1980 102 tonnes of containers were shipped to international destinations. Annual growth rose steadily culminating in 1,631 tonnes in 2014, a sixteen-fold increase.

Biodiversity and food
(pages 43–45)

1a   **a)** an organism **b)** a species **c)** a habitat **d)** a community **e)** an ecosystem
1b   Students' own answers.

2   **a)** die out **b)** add up to **c)** depend on **d)** provide us with **e)** guard against **f)** come about **g)** take on **h)** soak up
They are multi-word verbs (phrasal or prepositional verbs).

3   **Box 1** Three-word verbs
Box 2 Phrasal verbs (intransitive /does not take an object)
Box 3 Phrasal verbs (transitive / takes an object)
Box 4 Prepositional verbs
Box 5 Prepositional verbs (with two objects)

4a   Students' own answers.

4b   **Box 1** Three-word verbs: *keep up with, face up to*
Box 2 Phrasal verbs (intransitive): *speak out*
Box 3 Phrasal verbs (transitive): *leave X out, leave out X; point X out, point out X*
Box 4 Prepositional verbs: *come from X, rely on X*
Box 5 Prepositional verbs (with two objects): *supply X with*

5   **a)** Working out how (not ~~Working out that~~); looking after valuable ecosystems (not ~~looking valuable ecosystems after~~)
b) led to (not ~~led out~~); cutting them down (not ~~cutting down them~~)
c) dying out (not ~~die out~~); depriving future generations of (not ~~depriving future generations with~~)
d) coming up with initiatives (not ~~coming up initiatives~~); areas which are protected from (not ~~areas which are protected of~~)
e) turned into a symbol (not ~~turned it into a symbol~~); trying out new ingredients (not ~~trying out of new ingredients~~)

6   Students' own answers.

Megacities (pages 46–49)

1 **1** in /of **2** since, after, from **3** until, to **4** in **5** of **6** over / above **7** in / by **8** of **9** in, within, during, throughout, over **10** By / In **11** around, about **12** of **13** of **14** at **15** between **16** in **17** to **18** of They are all prepositions.

2 In 1970, the first three megacities were Tokyo (Japan), Osaka (Japan) and New York (USA).
The twenty-eight megacities in 2014 were:
1 Tokyo, Japan (37,833) 2 Delhi, India (24,953) 3 Shanghai, China (22,991) 4 Mexico City, Mexico (20,843) 5 Sao Paulo, Brazil (20,831) 6 Mumbai, India (20,741) 7 Osaka, Japan (20,123) 8 Beijing, China (19,520) 9 New York, USA (18,591) 10 Cairo, Egypt (18, 419) 11 Dhaka, Bangladesh (16,982) 12 Karachi, Pakistan (16,126) 13 Buenos Aires, Argentina (15,024) 14 Kolkata, India (14,766) 15 Istanbul, Turkey (13,954) 16 Chongqing, China (12,916) 17 Rio de Janeiro, Brazil (12,825) 18 Manila, Philippines (12,764) 19 Lagos, Nigeria (12,614) 20 Los Angeles, USA (12,308) 21 Moskva, Russia (12,063) 22 Guangzhou, Guangdong, China (11,843) 23 Kinshasa, Democratic Republic of the Congo (11,116) 24 Tianjin, China (10,860) 25 Paris, France (10,764) 26 Shenzhen, China (10,680) 27 London, UK (10,189) 28 Jakarta, Indonesia (10,176)
(*Figures from United Nations Department of Economic and Social Affairs / Population Division.*)

3 **1** different from **2** one in eight **3** at very different rates **4** on average **5** In contrast **6** availability of **7** proximity to **8** responsible for **9** effects on **10** crucial for **11** improvements in

4 **Box A** adjective + preposition
Box B noun + preposition
Box C prepositional phrase

5 Student's own answers.

6 The UNESCO Global Network of Learning Cities (GNLC) encourages cities to put education and lifelong learning **at** the heart of their development and become 'learning cities'. An initiative in Medellín, Colombia, has integrated education into urban planning **with** dramatic results. In the 1980s, Medellín was the headquarters of Pablo Escobar's drug cartel and infamous **for** its narcoterrorism and corruption. After Escobar's death in 1993, the city established a progressive agenda, involving communities in the expansion **of** public spaces and services. The programme included a metro system, innovative buildings and parks which doubled **as** learning spaces, and the construction of 120 new public schools.
It is Mayor Sergio Fajardo **to** whom much of the success of the initiative has been attributed. **Under** his visionary leadership, Medellin has been transformed into one of the most innovative cities in the world. As a result there has been a dramatic decrease **in** the incidence of crime and violence. To reduce inequality, Fajardo focused **on** improving public education, rather than supporting private education. Over the past two decades, the government allocated **up** to 40% of its municipal budget to education. The investment programme targeted the poorest areas providing a message of public support in a place once belonging **to** crime gangs.

7 Students' own answers.

Sensational news (pages 50–53)

1 Students' own answers.

2 It shows that the media is quick to report on sensational stories but very slow to qualify them or correct their own mistakes.

3a

manner	unfavourably
place	at a US government conference, in Washington
time (including duration)	over the last decade, three days later, immediately, between September 20th and September 28th
frequency	usually
degree of certainty (possibility and probability)	probably
viewpoint	apparently

3b **1** Adverbs of time and place usually come at the end of a clause, but are sometimes used **at the start**.
2 Adverbs of frequency and adverbs which refer to a degree of certainty often go **in mid-position**.
3 Adverbs of viewpoint are used **in mid-position**, but they can also be used at the start of a sentence since they may refer to the whole idea.

4 **1** c **2** g **3** b **4** f **5** e **6** d **7** a

5 **a)** 4 **b)** 1 **c)** 5 **d)** 2 **e)** 3

6 **1** place the focus **2** similar **3** surprising **4** a short time ago **5** in mid-position **6** object

7 **1** Sensationalism is definitely nothing new.
2 Also, criticism of sensationalism has a long history. / Criticism of sensationalism also has a long history. (*has* is used here as a main verb, not as an auxiliary verb, so the adverb precedes it. An example of *has* used as an auxiliary verb would be *The damage has been done.*)
3 Even the Roman philosopher Cicero complained / The Roman philosopher Cicero even complained
4 only reported the latest gossip about gladiators / reported only the latest gossip about gladiators
5 and frequently neglected to report real news
6 probably for reasons of natural selection
7 particularly those involving relationships and danger
8 Arguably, sensationalism promotes the spread of information / Sensationalism arguably promotes the spread of information
9 While some of the stories are scarcely believable
10 others actually help us to establish
11 the sugary dessert that you devour eagerly / the sugary dessert that you eagerly devour
12 it's quite bad for you
13 you can always have a salad tomorrow
14 is just a quality that is very human / is a quality that is just very human

8 **1** only **2** accurately **3** relatively **4** steadily **5** consistently **6** clearly **7** extremely **8** significantly **9** largely

9 **Sample answer**

The media is very quick to report sensational stories, such as world disasters, the personal failings of public figures and crime. Readers and viewers relate to the human aspects of these stories. However, there are other important stories which do not receive an equal amount of media coverage.

In the event of a major disaster, news reporting is dominated by information about the incident. There is a great deal of repetition in the reports and the smallest details are magnified out of proportion. Arguably, this is a cynical attempt on the part of news channels and websites to draw in readers and viewers. At such times, we hear very little other news. There are even claims that unpopular news is often deliberately released when the public is distracted by a more sensational story. Especially now that there are so many ways to access the news, the role of news agencies should be to inform the public about all news and not only what they consider the public needs to hear.

There are some very important issues about which we hear practically nothing. Many people in poorer nations suffer because of health issues that could be cured with relatively basic healthcare. International aid from wealthier nations is surprisingly low and yet this is not something we often hear about. To get accurate information on stories like this you usually have to consult the websites of non-profit-making organisations. Mainstream news organisations should be making this information available to us instead.

Personally, I believe that we should take more advantage of the increasing availability of information to make sure that the news we receive is unbiased, objective and covers all aspects of life in our world today.

The skills of a locksmith (pages 54–57)

1 Locksmith and silversmith are professions. A locksmith makes and repairs locks and security systems for homes, businesses and cars. A silversmith makes jewellery and other things out of silver. A songsmith is a person who is good at writing songs. A wordsmith is a person who is clever at using language.

2a **a)** good carpentry and metalwork skills, good motor skills, computer skills, specialised qualifications
b) Contact the MLA for further information.
c) Set up in business without qualifications.
d) strong obligation: *must (not), have to*; necessity: *need*; advice: *should*

2b *must* and *should* are pure modal verbs.
have to expresses a similar idea to must but behaves as an ordinary verb.
need sometimes behaves as a modal verb, but not in this example.

2c **a)** without 'to'
b) do not add -s
c) without
d) after

3 **1** interpersonal skills **2** stressful **3** Academic **4** knowledge **5** professional **6** general public

4 **1** A locksmith must not pass their skills onto the general public.
2 Locksmiths do not have to obtain an academic degree.
3 You ought to keep up-to-date with new products and developments in security technology.
4 They need good interpersonal skills.

5 They need to have current expert knowledge.
6 An alternative security measure must be put into place.
7 On occasion, a broken component needs replacing.

5 **1** Thieves are opportunists and **do not need** to be given much encouragement to try their luck.
2 You **don't have to** (= it isn't necessary to) leave lights on all day.
3 You **should use** a downstairs room with a drawn curtain and sufficient light inside to suggest that the room is occupied.
4 A light **shouldn't** be left on solely in the hall – it is not normal for the occupants to spend all night in the hall!
5 But for your house to be secure, you **must make sure / need to make sure** that your physical defences – the locks, the bars and window bolts - will resist attack.
6 Glass panels in doors **should be replaced** with laminated glass or reinforced with security film or grilles.
7 An internal cover plate **needs to be fitted** to letterboxes.
8 If your flat is on the second floor or above, y**ou need to balance** security with fire safety.
9 That means you shouldn't fit your front door with a lock that **needs** a key to open it from the inside.

6 **1** have needed to keep **2** did not need to pick **3** had to be opened **4** should have done **5** had to use **6** needn't have had

7 Students' own answers.

Eyewitness (pages 58–61)

1 **Suggested answers:**
Categorising words is a technique for helping memory. Because the second group of words can be easily grouped into categories, you can probably remember more of these words.
Factors that can affect the memorisation of these words: age, first language, distraction, anxiety.

2a Memorise as many words as you **can**.
Now cover the list and see how many words you **can** write down in two minutes.
However, it **can** be surprisingly difficult to remember them
How many words **could** you remember this time?
Other factors **can** affect the memorisation of these words too.
What factors **can** you think of?

2b *can* and *could* are modal verbs.
The grammatical features of modal verbs are:
Third person forms do not take *-s*.
Question forms do not require *do / does*.
Negatives are formed with *not*. Modal verbs are followed by infinitive without *to*.

2c **a)** These talk or ask about ability:
Memorise as many words as you can.
Cover the list and see how many words you can write down in two minutes.
How many words could you remember this time?
What factors can you think of?
b) These are statements that the writer believes to be true:
However, it can be surprisingly difficult to remember them.
Other factors can affect the memorisation of these words too.

3a **1** have not been able to **2** can often remember
3 succeeded in revealing **4** Both are possible.
5 Both are possible. **6** Both are possible.

3b Students' own answers.

4 Students' own answers.

5a An eyewitness is someone who sees an accident or crime and is able to describe it afterwards.

5b **may have seen, may be required:** these are different examples of the type of things an eyewitness sees or does and so are expressed as possibilities using *may*;

may be required is a passive form – it is not stated who requires this, but it is implied that this is 'by law'.

3 could be done: the writer is making a suggestion of what is possible in the future

4 can affect: the writer considers this to be true / a fact

5 (there) must be: the writer considers this to be highly probable / logical

6 There might be (another reason): the writer appears to consider this is only a possibility

7 may have been influenced: the writer thinks this was a possibility in the past; this is a passive form – the writer prefers to start this clause with the subject an (eyewitness's recall of events)

6 **Suggested answers:**
a) Sir Winston Churchill was Prime Minister twice, from 1940–45 and from 1951–55.
b) The window cleaner was cleaning the inside of the windows.

7 **Suggested answers:**
a) The man must work at the laboratory. He may have just fixed some of the equipment.
b) There must have been an accident. He could be dangerous.
c) Loftus argued that participants were less able to correctly recall the man with the knife because they were paying attention to the knife (presumably because it was potentially a source of danger to them), and so were distracted from the appearance of the man holding it. This has become known as 'weapon focus' and explains how witnesses to violent crimes may accurately recall central details (e.g. the type of weapon and what was done with it), but may be less accurate at recalling the appearance or clothing of the criminal.

8 **1** managed to describe **2** had been able to give / were able to give **3** could not have been predicted **4** must have experienced **5** could be / may be / might be **6** may even have read / might even have read / were even able to read / had even read **7** may not have been / might not have been / were not **8** may be affected **9** (can) recall **10** cannot / can't be controlled **11** therefore provide / can therefore provide / could therefore provide / may therefore provide

9 Students' own answers.

Early warning (pages 62–64)

1 **a)** flood
b) Sentence a is an example of a first conditional: if + present, will + infinitive without to. Sentence b is an example of a zero conditional: both clauses are in the present tense.
c) Real events or situations are ones that are possible now or in the future. Zero conditionals are often used to describe scientific facts: situations that always have the same results.

2 **1** c **2** a **3** d **4** b

3 **a)** a wild fire **b)** a hurricane **c)** a heatwave **d)** a volcanic eruption

4 **a)** The present simple tense is not always used in the *if*-clause of a first conditional sentence. In these examples, the present continuous (*If you are visiting*) is also used. Passive forms and the *be going to* future are also possible.
b) In item c, *provided that* is used instead of *if*.
c) In item b, the modal verb *should* is used instead of *will* to give advice; in item c, *can* is used to express possibility. You can also use the modals *may, might* and *could* to express greater doubt. An imperative form is used in item a. The *be going to* future can also be used instead of *will*.
d) A comma is only used after the *if*-clause when it comes first in the sentence.

5 Students' own answers.

6 **1** Not Given **2** True **3** False **4** True **5** False **6** True

7 **1** Had a reliable early warning system been in place in Myanmar, could the scale of the disaster have been reduced?
2 … unless a more people-centred approach were in place.
3 In addition, their capacity to evacuate the area would have been severely limited by poor roads and infrastructure.

8 **a)** Evidence suggests that if governments spent one US dollar on prevention, they would save four dollars on emergency response.
b) If people had been given enough time, they would / could have left their homes.
c) Poverty would be / would have been less severe in this area if people hadn't lost their livelihoods in the flood.
d) The government knew that unless the problems were addressed, the cycle of flood and famine would continue.
e) Even if an early warning system was / were in place, the effects of the cyclone would have been serious.
f) How much damage would have been caused if the cyclone had taken a different path? How much damage would have been caused had the cyclone taken a different path?

9 Students' own answers.

Online survey (pages 65–67)

1a **Suggested answers:**
a) A freelancer is someone who / that works independently.
b) A participant is someone who / that takes part in an activity.
c) Cloud-based computing is a type of computing which / that allows users to share information between different devices.
d) Customer feedback is advice which customers give a business on a product or service.

1b **1–3** who, which, that (in any order), **4&5** who, which (in any order), **6** who

2 **1** B **2** C **3** E **4** A **5** D **6** F

3a **a)** Without the relative clause, the definition of freelancers is not complete. It explains that they are highly skilled individuals but this could also apply to other people who are not freelance.
b) Without the relative clause, we don't have all the information we need. We don't know which specific two-week period is being referred to.
c) Without the relative clause, this sentence still makes sense. The relative clause adds extra information.

3b Sentences **a** and **b** contain defining relative clauses. Sentence **c** contains a non-defining relative clause.

4
a) This chart shows where the freelancers who responded to the Freelance Industry Report survey are based and the length of their working week.
b) The chart shows the average hours (which / that) the freelancers worked per week.
c) The graph, which shows the average hours worked every week by region, proves that freelancers are hardworking professionals.
d) One interesting fact is that freelancers in Australia (35%), South America (34%) and Europe (33%) are the most likely to work 40 or more hours per week, which shatters the myth that people in these regions don't typically work long hours.
e) Fewer hours were worked in North America and Asia, where people are generally thought to have long working weeks.
f) The participants, almost half of whom were designers, writers or editors, answered a range of questions.

5a&5b **a)** The anonymity ~~that~~ the internet provides makes it the ideal environment for asking customers their opinions about a business, product or service.
b) There are a number of websites where businesses can access software to create a simple online survey.
c) Surveys can be aimed at the general public or there may be a specific group of customers from whom a business wishes to get feedback.
d) There are many different types of questions ~~that are~~ used in a survey.
e) Most people taking part in surveys prefer short multiple-choice questions.
f) Participants don't have to fill in questions ~~which~~ they don't consider relevant to them.

6 **Sample answer:**
This diagram shows the stages used by an online survey provider to gather feedback for a client. First the survey is commissioned by the client. Once the questionnaires have been created, the survey provider contacts participants with invitations, which can be sent out by email. Reminders will be emailed at regular intervals until sufficient responses have been reached. Surveys completed by respondents will be emailed direct to the survey provider, who will respond with a thank you email. The survey provider is then responsible for analysing the data, which will be published as a report. The client who commissioned the survey will receive the report within four weeks of receiving the data.

Plastic ocean (pages 68–70)

1 Students' own answers.

2a Students' own answers.
2b active tense: *travels*, *mistake it*
passive tense: *has been left*, *is blown*, *is eaten*
relative clause: *which has been left*, *which mistakes it for food*
2c **1** left **2** mistaking
The words *mistaking* and *left* are both participles; *mistaking* is a present participle and *left* a past participle but these names are confusing as either can be used in present or past contexts. In this lesson we refer to present participles as *-ing* participles and past participles as *-ed* participles (*-ed* participles include both regular and irregular participles so *polluted* and *left* are both *-ed* participles).

3a **1** has been discarded **2** is broken down **3** are ingested **4** are known as **5** accumulates **6** and **7** is used, have been made

3b
a) They can make your writing more succinct and less repetitive.
b) The Grammar reference provides the examples *floating* and *polluted*. Other examples in the text are: *man-made*, *much-needed*, *pioneering*, *solar-powered*.
c) We use the *-ing* participle as an alternative to an active verb when the subject is the same in each clause. We use the *-ed* participle as an alternative to a passive form.
d) There are three: *Once discarded, … After breaking down … , when ingested, …*

4 **Suggested answers:**
a) A new species of bacteria, discovered by Japanese scientists, is able to consume one of the world's most common plastics.
b) Being both lightweight and strong, PET is widely used to make disposable water bottles. / Widely used to make disposable water bottles, PET is both lightweight and strong.
c) Published in the journal *Science*, the discovery could be a breakthrough in managing the plastic. / The discovery, published in the journal *Science,* could be a breakthrough in managing the plastic.
d) Scientists collected 250 PET-contaminated samples, including sediment, soil and wastewater, from a plastic bottle recycling site.
e) On / When screening / Screening the microbes living on the samples, scientists found just one of the bacteria species, named *Ideonella sakaiensis*, was responsible for PET degradation.
f) Further tests revealed the bacteria used enzymes to break down the PET, generating an intermediate chemical.
g) The chemical was then taken up by the cell, where it was broken down even further by other enzymes, providing the bacteria with carbon and energy to grow.
h) If kept at a temperature of 29°C, a community of *Ideonella sakaiensis* could break down a thin film of PET in just six weeks. / A community of *Ideonella sakaiensis* could break down a thin film of PET in just six weeks if kept at a temperature of 29°C.

5 **1** creating **2** fall **3** catches **4** housed **5** containing **6** acting**,** forcing **7** escapes

6 **Suggested answer:**
Plastic bottles are taken to the bottle bank to be recycled. From there, they are transported to a factory. The sorting process at the factory is done by hand, separating the bottles into different colours or types of plastic and discarding larger pieces of rubbish, such as stones. The plastic bottles are then shredded into smaller pieces of plastic. Next the plastic is washed, removing labels and glue. The clean plastic is heated, which when melted, is turned into small pellets. The pellets are dropped into a machine which heats the plastic to 600°F so that it can be moulded. The finished product is a disposable water bottle.